MW00426997

In the Name of Allah,
Most Compassionate,
Most Merciful

al-Asmā'ul-Husnā

The 99 Beautiful Names of Allah

M. R. Bawa Muhaiyaddeen

THE FELLOWSHIP PRESS
Philadelphia, PA

Library of Congress Catalog Card Number: 79-19619
ISBN: 0-914390-13-9

Printed in the United States of America
by THE FELLOWSHIP PRESS
Bawa Muhaiyaddeen Fellowship

First Printing 1979
Second Printing 1989
Third Printing 1993
Fourth Printing 1997
Fifth Printing 2002

Muhammad Raheem Bawa Muhaiyaddeen (Ral.)

The *Asmā'ul-Husnā* is the wealth of Allah, the power of Allah, the actions of Allah, the virtuous qualities of Allah, and the virtuous behavior of Allah. The totality of everything is condensed and brought into action within these duties.

from *Asmā'ul-Husnā*

Contents

EDITOR'S NOTE TO THE SECOND EDITION

The transliteration of the ninety-nine names has been revised to conform with more commonly used standards. The glossary and written text, however, remain as originally published in the first edition.

Introduction

This is a small and simple explanation about God and His duties, about what are known as the 99 Holy Names of God, or the *Asmā'ul-Husnā* of Allah. The meanings of these names are endless, limitless, and indescribable. Even if all the water in the seas were made into ink and the wood from all the forests in the world were made into pens to write with, we could not finish writing the explanations of these beautiful attributes of God. They are the power of God; they are His attributes known as grace. They are the duties which God performs; they are His qualities.

His story cannot be fully written. This is only an explanation of a particle, the minutest of minute particles, of that duty. This world is a dot [*nuqat*]. The 18,000 universes are just a dot of His limitless power and duty. That dot, which is creation, is all that we see. That dot is so small, but if it were split into hundreds and hundreds of millions of pieces,

1

and if we took one tiny, minute point from it, then this explanation would be just that small point. It is only this small point that our wisdom can understand. Not even those with more wisdom could ever fully explain the *Asmā'ul-Husnā*. No one, not even the very learned, can find an end to this. Each can only give an explanation according to his own state of wisdom.

Here I have given a minute explanation about His duty, according to the capacity understood by my wisdom. Another person may be able to understand and analyze beyond this, according to the wisdom that he has. The explanation given here is from the wisdom of the smallest of small ants. My wisdom is like the wisdom of the tiny red ants in Ceylon, and this explanation is given according to that wisdom.

The total meaning of the *Asmā'ul-Husnā* cannot be revealed to the wisdom of man. Yet there is this wonder: to whomever asks, an explanation will be given according to his state, according to his ideas, and according to his mind. I will answer according to the state in which the question is asked. It is not something which belongs to oneself. For the same question, there will be an explanation appropriate to each child; to a child in a different state, there will be a different answer. Each time more and more will be revealed. If there is yet another child, the answer will be different again. The explanation will be given according to the potential understanding of the questioner. As one's wisdom and purity develop, deeper and deeper meanings will be revealed. There cannot be a fixed answer. The total meaning of the *Asmā'ul-Husnā* has no limit. This is only an explanation given according to the capacity of those who were there. The treasury of God is like that; it will explain according to the capacity of those who are listening. These are very short explanations; they are not very long, but they will enter within the *qalb* [the innermost heart].

You must try to pronounce these words and intend their meaning correctly. God is the trustee, He is the law, He is the judge. Allah decides who is speaking these words correctly and who is not. Allah looks only at the *qalb* of the one who is reciting; He does not look at the words being said. He looks only at the *qalb*. One who is learned will look at the letters, but Allah looks at the *qalbs*. For one who is not learned, it is his *qalb* which speaks. Allah looks at that clarity. Allah does not look to see if the letters are clear or if the pronunciation is clear. He looks only to see if the heart is clear.

One who is learned *should* recite correctly. If he knows how but does not speak clearly, there is punishment for him. A learned man must pronounce the vowels and the consonants correctly. But Allah will understand the unlearned man; Allah alone will understand his faith. The unlearned man will know only one word—Allah. His whole life and existence will be concentrated on Allah alone. Within his faith, he can recite in any manner, because his heart is watched by Allah alone. Allah revealed this point at the time of the Rasool (Sal.), [1] when Bilal (Ral.) [2] and a learned man both recited the call to prayer. It is because of this incident that Allah declared, "It is I alone who knows and accepts the prayers of my servants!" Allah has said, "Prayer belongs to Me. I am the One who accepts prayer. I am the One who gives judgment, and I am the One who provides food for all My creations. I alone can do this. No one else can do this work. I am the One responsible." Allah is the only One to whom this *Asmā'ul-Husnā* applies. There is no one equal to Allah; there is no one who can be compared to Allah. Therefore, no one other than Allah can find fault in the pronunciation or recitation.

---

[1] Rasool: The Messenger, Muhammad (Sal.).

(Sal.)—The shortened form of *Sallallāhu 'alaihi wa sallam*: May God bless him and grant him eternal peace. A supplication traditionally spoken after mentioning the name of Prophet Muhammad (Sal.).

[2] (Ral.)—The shortened form of *Radhiyallāhu 'anhu*: May Allah be pleased with him. A supplication traditionally spoken after mentioning the name of a saint or *khalifah*.

The story of Bilāl (Ral.) referred to here can be found in *God, His Prophets and His Children*, by His Holiness Bawa Muhaiyaddeen.

One who is learned must ask forgiveness of Allah for his mistakes. Allah alone can grant that forgiveness. It is like that. The one who is unlearned has faith; his *qalb* is his Qur'an. The faith of his *qalb* is his recitation, faith is his clear pronunciation and that clarity of faith is his prayer. Such is the search of the unlearned man. He recites through his heart. He has absolute trust [*tawakkul*] in Allah alone. He has only one point, and that point is Allah. His focus is, "Allah, Rasool, Allah, Rasool, Allah, Rasool!" That is what he will say. But the learned man has many points; he is not focused in one state. His *qalb* contains more than one state. To correct his faults, he must ask God for forgiveness and then correct himself. Forgiveness cannot be asked from anyone else. It must be asked from Allah.

There is another *hadīsz* [tradition]: If anybody hurts the heart of one who is an *Insān Kāmil* (one who is a slave to Allah, one who is a *mu'min* or a true believer), Allah cannot bear it. Whether learned people or ordinary people hurt the heart of such a one, Allah cannot bear it or grant forgiveness. If you ask forgiveness from Allah in that instance, He will say, "Ask forgiveness from the one you have hurt." In that instance, you will have to ask forgiveness from the slave of God. As soon as his *qalb* is made peaceful, then Allah's *qalb* will be made peaceful, and Allah's love will be peaceful.

However, if you hurt the heart of an ordinary person, then it is good to ask forgiveness from him as soon as you realize your fault, but still you must also ask forgiveness from God. Otherwise, the punishment for your actions will come to you on Judgment Day. But the punishment for hurting a slave of God will come to you immediately; it is like falling into a fire. That is the meaning of this *hadīsz*.

Now, let us read the list of the attributes of Allah. After that, we will explain a little further.

الْأَسْمَاءُ الْحُسْنَى

al-Asmā'ul-Husnā

يَآ اَللّهُ

yā Allāh

GOD, THE ONE AND ONLY.

He is within Himself in His own hands. His duty is the protection, preservation, and salvation of creation. He generates things which are with and without wisdom and makes them become useful things. He creates everything, but nothing is equal to Him.

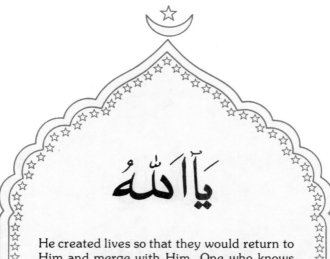

يَآ اللهُ

He created lives so that they would return to Him and merge with Him. One who knows Him will merge with Him in the end, and such a one is given the power and grace for that state. For earth, heaven, seas, rain, hills, for things with and without life, even for atoms and un-atoms, He gives His grace which is all-perfection. Not lacking anything, He is endless, birthless, and deathless. He exists always, granting grace. Finally, He calls for praise and that comes. He has endless rays and compassion. That name, *Yā Allāhu*, is in His hand. In this state, His praise and glory are in His own hands. No one else can know it. This name of His grace is only one point of His grace.

1

يَا رَحْمٰنُ

ya Raḥmān

THE MERCIFUL
The Compassionate, Most Gracious,
Beneficent, Kind, and
Understanding; The Cherisher.

Explanation: The One who has endless compassion for all lives. He is compassionate
and helpful to all lives.

2

يَا رَحِيْمُ

yā Raḥīm

THE COMPASSIONATE
The Most Merciful, Clement, Kind,
and Understanding; The Sustainer
and Redeemer.

Explanation: The One who is full of endless
compassion for all lives.

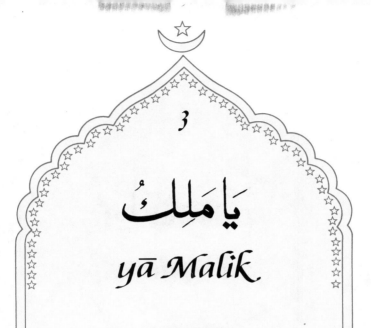

3

يَا مَلِكُ

yā Malik

THE KING
The Sovereign, King of Kings,
Monarch, Possessor.

Explanation: The king of the utmost interior
and exterior of all creation. He is the king
that discharges help and justice to all.

4

يَا قُدُّوسُ

yā Quddūs

THE HOLY
The Most Holy, All-Holy.

Explanation: The Holy of holies of all creation. The holiest. The One without dirt, scars, or guilt. The purest.

5

يَا سَلَامُ

yā Salām

THE PEACE
The Source of Peace and Perfection;
The Bringer of Safety, Security,
Intactness, and Well-Being.

Explanation: The One who gives His grace,
purifies His creation, and tries to draw it to
Himself. The One who has that grace and
compassion.

6

يَا مُؤْمِنُ

yā Mu'min

THE FAITHFUL
The Guardian of Faith,
Keeper or Giver of Faith,
Bestower of Security.

Explanation: The One who protects all of
creation by His compassion and grace.

7

يَا مُهَيْمِنُ

yā Muhaimin

THE PROTECTOR
The Guardian, Preserver of Safety,
Helper of Those in Peril, The Master.

Explanation: The One who looks into every
creation by the light of His grace and helps
them.

8

يَا عَزِيزُ

yā 'Azīz

THE MIGHTY

The Strong and Powerful; The Exalted
in Might; The Respected, Noble,
Valuable, and Beloved Friend.

Explanation: The all-powerful and all-grace-
ful God. The One who has created all of
creation, but has created none equal to Himself. He protects His creations and saves
them.

٩

يَاجَبَّارُ

yā Jabbār

THE REPAIRER
The Restorer; The Irresistible,
All-Compelling, Omnipotent,
and Almighty.

Explanation: The One who makes imperfect
things in creation perfect.

10

يَامُتَكَبِّرُ

yā Mutakabbir

THE SELF-EXPANDING
The Self-Magnifying; The Supreme,
Majestic, and Dignified;
The Great One.

Explanation: The One who creates and who
is compassion. The One who has no equal in
praise or power.

يَاخَالِقُ

yā Khaliq

THE CREATOR
The Originator, The Maker.

Explanation: The One who has created all creations and sustains them.

12

يَا بَارِئُ

yā Bāri'

THE MAKER FROM NOTHING
The Creator, The Producer of Souls.

Explanation: The One who has the grace of creating all creation.

13

يَامُصَوِّرُ

yā Muṣawwir

THE FASHIONER
The Shaper, Bestower of Forms,
Creator of Lives.

Explanation: The One who gives physical
power to all creation and who has the power
to give physical form to all creation.

14

يَاغَفَّارُ

yā G͟haffār

THE ABSOLVER
The Forgiver, The Pardoner.

Explanation: The One who is patient and forgives the faults of all creation and those of His slaves.

15

يَا قَهَّارُ

yā Qahhār

THE DOMINANT
The Subduer, Conqueror,
Supreme, Almighty.

Explanation: The One who creates, promotes, increases, and decreases. The One who has the power to do so.

16

يَاوَهَّابُ

yā Wahhāb

THE BESTOWER
The Giver.

Explanation: The One who gives free wages to all creations, even though the creation does not do the work of God.

17

يَا رَزَّاقُ

yā Razzāq

THE PROVIDER
The Sustainer and Maintainer,
The Bestower of Sustenance.

Explanation: The One who gives food to all creations according to the capacity and need of their stomachs.

18

يَا فَتَّاحُ

yā Fattāḥ

THE OPENER OF THE HEART
The Granter of Success,
The Reliever.

Explanation: The One who grants whatever is asked according to the longings of the heart.

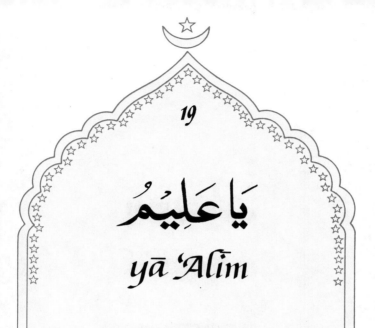

19

يَا عَلِيْمُ

yā 'Alim

THE OMNISCIENT
The All-Knowing.

Explanation: The One who knows the inner-most heart of all creations.

20

يَاقَابِضُ

yā Qābiḍ

THE RESTRAINER
The Constrainer, Seizer,
Catcher, Withholder.

Explanation: You are the One who reduces
the daily food of those of Your creations that
forget You and think that they are feeding
themselves through their own effort; and
You make them realize their faults.

21

يَابَاسِطُ

yā Bāsiṭ

THE SPREADER
The Extender, Unfolder, Embracer.

Explanation: When Your creations seek You and ask You, You give them food, open their hearts, and save them with Your grace.

22

يَاخَافِضُ

yā Khāfiḍ

THE ABASER
The Humbler.

Explanation: The One who humiliates those who have forgotten You, resisted You, or hated You. By giving diseases and poverty, You make them realize and then draw them to Yourself.

23

يَا رَافِعُ

yā Rafiʿ

THE EXALTER
The Upraiser.

Explanation: The One who promotes all His creations according to the state of their *Īmān* [absolute faith, certitude, and determination].

24

يَا مُعِزُّ

yā Mu'izz

THE HONORER
The Strengthener, Exalter,
The Raiser to Honor.

Explanation: The One who purifies in this
world and the next world those creations
who have Īmān.

25

يَا مُذِلُّ

yā Mudhill

THE DEGRADER
The Humiliator, Abaser, Dishonorer.

Explanation: The One who sends to hell those who have forgotten Him and instead have followed satan.

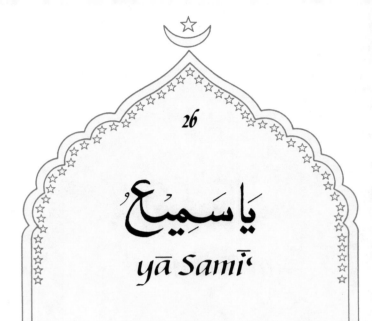

26

يَا سَمِيعُ

yā Samī'

THE ALL-HEARING
The Hearer.

Explanation: Out of creation, those with holy hearts pray to You. If it is good, You grant them Your grace.

27

يَا بَصِيرُ

yā Baṣīr

THE ALL-SEEING
The Seer, The All-Comprehending.

Explanation: God, who through His divine
grace, sees the within and the without of
every creation.

28

يَا حَكَمُ

yā Ḥakam

THE JUDGE
The Giver of True Justice,
The Arbitrator.

Explanation: God, knowing good and evil deeds, give final judgment.

29

يَا عَدْلُ

yā ʾAdl

THE EQUITABLE
The Just, The Impartial.

Explanation: God, knowing the good and evil deeds in the _qalb_ [the innermost heart] of each creation, dispenses compassionate justice.

30

يَالَطِيفُ

yā Laṭīf

**THE MOST SUBTLE
AND GRACIOUS**
The Kind, Refined, Gentle, and
Most Pleasant; The Mysterious;
The Knower of the Most
Subtle Mysteries.

Explanation: God, knowing the inner *qalb* of
each creation, endows them with divine
goodness.

31

يَا خَبِيرُ

yā Khabīr

THE AWARE
The Experienced, The Knowing.

Explanation: God, who knows the secrets in the inner recesses of the life, wisdom, and mind of each creation.

32

يَا حَلِيمُ

yā Ḥalīm

THE CLEMENT
The Mild, Gentle, Forbearant,
and Patient.

Explanation: God endows the qualities and
action of each creation with patience and forbearance.

33

يَا عَظِيمُ

yā 'Aẓīm

THE SUPREME GLORY
The Magnificent, Superb, and Most
Important; The Mighty Splendor.

Explanation: God is infinitely greater in
wisdom than all His creations.

34

يَاغَفُورُ

yā Ghafūr

THE MUCH-FORGIVING
The Pardoner, The Forgiver.

Explanation: God, who exercises infinite forbearance, tolerance, and forgiveness toward the evil deeds of His creations.

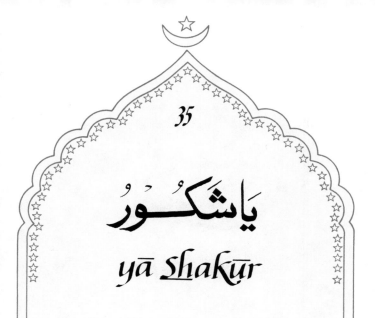

35

يَاشَكُورُ

yā _Shakūr_

THE MOST GRATEFUL
The Most Thankful.

Explanation: God, who assists and helps every creation who goes in search of Him. He protects, blesses, and guides always.

36

يَا عَلِيُّ

yā 'Aliy

THE EXALTED
The Most High, Sublime, Supreme.

Explanation: God is the only One above all
creations who exists forever in His glory.

يَا كَبِيرُ

yā Kabīr

THE GREAT
The Vast, Venerable,
and Formidable.

Explanation: God is the greatest power in
the entirety of His creation.

38

يَاحَفِيظُ

yā Ḥafīẓ

THE PRESERVER
The Protector, Guardian,
Sustainer, Defender.

Explanation: God preserves, protects, and
guides each and every one in creation.

39

يَا مُقِيتُ

yā Muqīt

THE SUSTAINER
The Nourisher, Maintainer,
Provider, Supporter, Feeder,
and Strengthener.

Explanation: God, who endows strength and
resolution to each of His creations and sup-
plies them with firmness and determination.

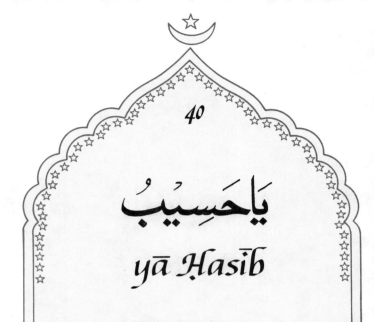

40

يَاحَسِيبُ

yā Ḥasīb

THE RECKONER
The Calculator, The Esteemed
and Noble.

Explanation: God, who will call for the account of good and evil deeds on Judgment Day.

41

يَا جَلِيْلُ

yā Jalil

THE SUBLIME
The Glorious and Benign;
The Resplendent,
Majestic, and Honorable.

Explanation: God neither needs nor will
accept an atom of the material earnings,
wealth, or strength of any of His creation.

42

يَا كَرِيمُ

yā Karīm

THE GENEROUS
The Bountiful, Noble, Beneficent,
Kind, and Precious One.

Explanation: God, who in His grace endows
each of His creations with the priceless heri-
tage of the soul and wisdom, and gives His
love as a reward according to the wisdom of
such a created soul.

43

يَا رَقِيبُ

yā Raqīb

THE WATCHFUL
The Guardian, Keeper, Observer,
Overseer, and Watcher.

Explanation: God, who looks at His created
beings through His penetrating divine rays.

44

يَا مُجِيبُ

yā Mujib

THE HEARER AND ANSWERER
OF PRAYER
The Granter, Accepter, Approver,
and Fulfiller of Prayer;
The Responsive.

Explanation: God, who accepts prayers and
grants them accordingly.

45

يَا وَاسِعُ

yā Wāsi'

THE COMPREHENSIVE
The Vast and Extensive,
All-Comprehending and
All-Containing.

Explanation: God, who knows the intentions
in the *qalb* of each creation and satisfies
them accordingly.

46

يَاحَكِيمُ

yā Ḥakīm

THE WISE
The Judicious, The Sagacious.

Explanation: Each creation of God will not
be able to gauge the extent, depth, and
greatness of His glory.

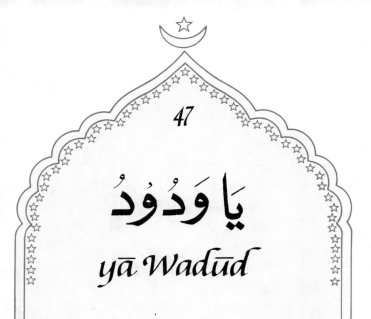

47

يَا وَدُودُ

yā Wadūd

THE LOVING
The Affectionate.

Explanation: Each creation of God comes within the embrace of His compassionate grace.

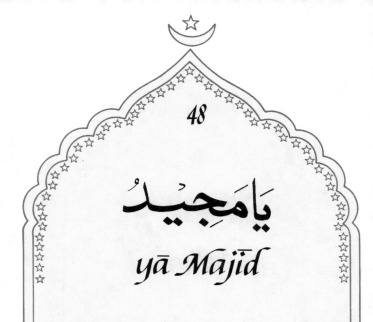

48

يَامَجِيدُ

yā Majīd

THE GLORIOUS
The Splendid and Praiseworthy.

Explanation: God is the sovereign ruler of every created being.

49

يَا بَاعِثُ

ya Bā'ith

THE RESURRECTOR
The Raiser from the Dead,
The Awakener and Sender-Forth,
The Reason and Cause.

Explanation: God, who has the supreme
power of reviving the dead and giving death
to those who are alive.

50

يَاشَهِيدُ

yā <u>Sh</u>ahīd

THE WITNESS
The Certifier.

Explanation: God, who appears before His creations who earnestly search for Him.

51

يَاحَقُّ

yā Ḥaqq

THE TRUTH
The Reality, The Duty,
The Just and Correct.

Explanation: Whatever difficulties, troubles, and hostile actions are engendered by creations toward God, they cannot disturb His infinite composure and strength.

52

يَا وَكِيْلُ

yā Wakīl

THE TRUSTEE
The Advocate, The Guardian.

Explanation: God, in His infinite compassion, bestows food to each creation whether it does good or evil deeds.

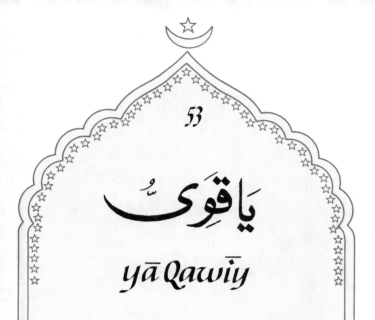

53

يَاقَوِىُّ

yā Qawīy

THE ALMIGHTY
The Forceful, Mighty, and Firm.

Explanation: God will crush through His infinite resolution, firmness, and strength whatever destruction, upheavals, or battles occur.

54

يَا مَتِينُ

yā Matīn

THE FIRM
The Strength of Determination,
The Steady.

Explanation: God, through His infinite grace, controls the waywardness and carelessness of the minds of His creations and looks toward them with infinite compassion.

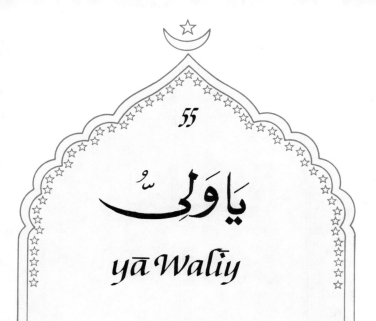

55

يَا وَلِيُّ

yā Walīy

THE NEAREST FRIEND
The Protector, Helper,
Patron, and Owner.

Explanation: God, seeing the true effulgence in the *qalb* of each being, offers
divine grace and gives them whatever they
need or require.

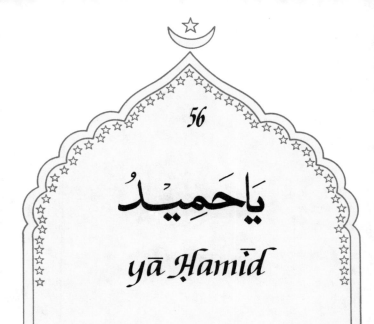

56

يَاحَمِيدُ

yā Ḥamīd

THE PRAISEWORTHY
The Laudable, The Benign.

Explanation: God, who glorifies the truth, wisdom, and *Īmān* of His true devotees.

57

يَا مُحْصِى

yā Muḥṣī

THE ACCOUNTANT
The Counter, The Reckoner.

Explanation: God envelops the *qalbs* of His true devotees with His limitless divine grace in order to protect their spotless effulgence.

58

يَامُبْدِئُ

yā Mubdi'

THE ORIGINATOR
The Beginner, Commencer,
and Founder.

Explanation: God, the Omnipotent, who
creates all lives and beings and ensures their
protection always.

59

يَا مُعِيدُ

yā Mu'id

THE RESTORER
The Resuscitator,
The Reviver of the Dead.

Explanation: God, who restores life over and over again to those who are dead, and it is He who passes judgment.

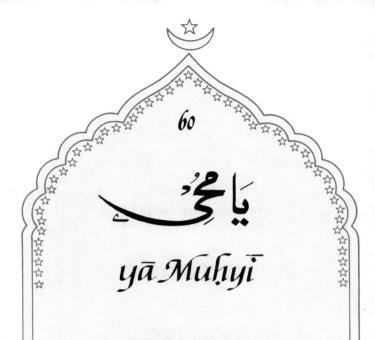

60

يَا مُحْيِ

yā Muḥyī

THE BESTOWER OF LIFE
The Quickener and Reviver.

Explanation: God, who restores life over and over again to those who are dead.

يَا مُمِيتُ

yā Mumīt

THE CAUSER OF DEATH
The Giver of Death, The Destroyer.

Explanation: God sends death to each and every created being according to divine decree. Thereafter, judgment is passed on Judgment Day according to good and evil deeds.

62

يَا حَيُّ

yā Ḥayy

THE LIVING
The Ever-Living and Everlasting.

Explanation: God, who exists in *anāthi* [the beginningless beginning], *āthi* [the time of the dawning of the light], and *awwal* [the beginning of creation], in this world and in the next world. He is forever existing, and He gives His infinite compassion to His entire creation.

63

يَا قَيُّوْمُ

yā Qayyūm

THE SELF-SUBSISTING

The Self-Existing,
The One Who Stands Alone,
The Firm and Steadfast.

Explanation: In order to protect all His created beings, God is vigilant and always resolute.

64

يَا وَاجِدُ

yā Wājid

THE FINDER
The All-Perceiving, The Inventor
and Maker.

Explanation: God does not need or desire
the least material good of the entire world.
God has only divine attributes, He needs no
earthly goods. Further, He bestows His
divine grace within the material things that
He does not need.

65

يَامَاجِدُ

yā Mājid

THE NOBLE
The Generous, The Glorious
and Sublime.

Explanation: God, who bestows infinite
compassion both within and without each
created being.

66

يَا وَاحِدُ

yā Waḥid

THE ONE
The Unique One, The Solitary One,
The Incomparable, The Singular,
The One Alone.

Explanation: God, who is alone perpetually
and who rules over the entire creation under
one divine umbrella.

67

يَاۤاَحَدُ

yā Aḥad

THE ONLY ONE
The One, The One Full of Grace,
The Secret One.

Explanation: God, who alone has the inalien-
able right to create, preserve, protect, and
rule over every created being. Everything
exists as His path of *Aḥad* [Secret of Unity].
In a state of *Īmān-Islām* [purity and surrender to God], *Insān Kāmil* [perfected man]
will know this *Aḥad*. The *Aḥad* exists as the
Resonance of Allah in all of everything.

68

يَا صَمَدُ

yā Ṣamad

THE ETERNAL-ABSOLUTE
The Eternal, Everlasting, Equality.

Explanation: God, who does not need or desire anything from any of His creations. Existing in all lives, He is the One who will be the peacefulness and will be the equality which treats everything equally. Holding other lives as one's own life, understanding and accepting the energies of all lives, He is the One who gives the explanation. He is the One who has created patience, tolerance, and peacefulness. He is the One who is justice.

69

يَا قَادِرُ

yā Qādir

THE POWERFUL
The Potent and Capable Master,
The Able One.

Explanation: God, who has the supreme
power to create, preserve, control, and
destroy every creation.

70

يَا مُقْتَدِرُ

yā Muqtadir

THE POSSESSOR OF POWER
The Possessor of Strength;
The Dominant, Prevailing, Able,
and Capable One.

Explanation: God, who always exhibits His
divine grace to the world through His authen-
tic devotees.

yā Muqaddim

THE FOREMOST

The Ancient, Infinitely Pre-Existent
and Sempiternal; The Offerer
and Giver; The Leader, Advancer,
and Preceder; The Expediter
and Promoter.

Explanation: God, knowing the spotless
purity of the *qalb* in each created being,
makes them divinely resplendent through
His grace.

72

يَا مُؤَخِّرُ

yā Mu'akhkhir

THE DEFERRER
The Delayer, Retarder, Postponer,
Terminator, The Last Remaining.

Explanation: God makes those who go forward on the evil dark path of satan go back-
ward from that path through His divine
grace. God does not allow the emergence of
evil qualities and stops them from arising.

73

يَاآَوَّلُ

yā Awwal

THE FIRST
The Beginning and The Foremost.

Explanation: God, who is firm toward all created beings, renders to each of them their needs and requirements.

74

يَاۤ اَخِرُ

yā Ākhir

THE LAST
The End and The Ultimate.

Explanation: God was first and foremost when creation was ushered in, is behind after all creation has come into existence, and will remain after the entire creation has ceased to exist.

75

يَاظَاهِرُ

yā Ẓāhir

THE MANIFEST
The Evident, Clear, Obvious,
Conspicuous, Outward, and External.

Explanation: God emerged through all His
creations in divine resplendence and with
His divine grace.

76

يَا بَاطِنُ

yā Bāṭin

THE HIDDEN
The Internal, The Inmost Secret.

Explanation: God, who is beyond the reach of both those who use an intermediary to approach Him and those who have doubts and suspicion within their hearts.

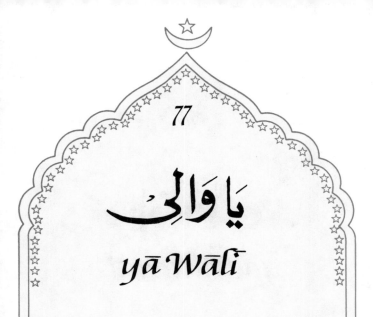

77

يَا وَالِي

ya Walī

THE GOVERNOR
The Friendly and Protecting Ruler.

Explanation: God, the Father of divine wisdom, inculcates the divine truths within the *qalb* of each creation.

78

يَا مُتَعَالِي

yā Muta'ālī

THE SUPREMELY EXALTED
The Most High.

Explanation: God, the One of limitless majesty and glory, and who cannot be calculated, determined, or understood by any of His creation.

79

يَا بَرُّ

yā Barr

THE RIGHTEOUS
The Dutiful and Devoted, The Kind
and Benign Benefactor.

Explanation: God bestows all good things
through His infinite divine compassion with
no advantage to Himself.

80

يَا تَوَّابُ

yā Tawwāb

THE ACCEPTOR OF REPENTANCE
The Forgiver, The Cause of
Repentance, The Merciful.

Explanation: God, who accepts the earnest
appeals of created beings possessed of a
spotless effulgent *qalb.*

81

يَا مُنْتَقِمُ

yā Muntaqim

THE AVENGER.

Explanation: God inflicts punishment on those who injure the *qalb* of spotless effulgence within His created beings.

82

يَا عَفُوُّ

yā 'Afūw

THE PARDONER
The Forgiving, Forbearant, Tolerant,
Indulgent, and Merciful One.

Explanation: God, who forgives and bestows
compassion on His creations who commit
mistakes in their ignorance.

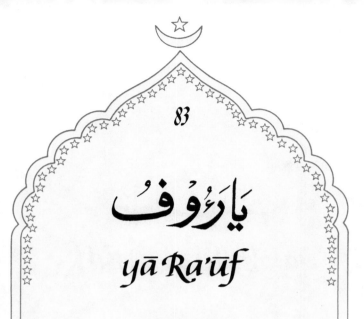

83

يَا رَؤُوفُ

yā Ra'uf

THE KIND
The Ever-Indulgent, Compassionate,
and Merciful; The Pitying
and Consoling One.

Explanation: God always bestows His infinite compassion and love to all lives of His
created beings.

84

يَامَالِكَ ٱلْمُلْكِ

yā Mālikal-Mulk

THE KING OF
SUPREME DOMINION
The Ruler, The King of All Kingdoms.

Explanation: God, who is always the Supreme Sovereign Ruler of both earth and heaven.

يَا ذَا الْجَلَالِ وَالْاِكْرَامِ

yā Dhal-Jalāli wal-Ikrām

THE LORD OF MAJESTY, GLORY, AND HONOR
The Lord of Majesty and Liberality.

Explanation: God bestows to all His created beings all they need in abundance. He gives them food and all they require according to their needs. This goes on perpetually.

86

يَا مُقْسِطُ

yā Muqsiṭ

THE JUST
The Equitable.

Explanation: God dispenses divine justice to
His created beings and protects them with
meticulous precision.

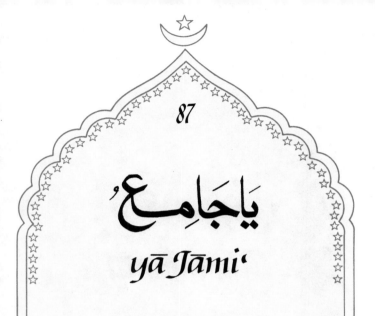

87

يَاجَامِعُ

yā Jami'

THE GATHERER
The Collector, The Assembler of All,
The Uniter, The Universal One.

Explanation: God will embrace all His created beings in compassionate love at the end
of the world.

88

يَا غَنِيُّ

yā G͟haniy

THE RICH
The Wealthy, The Independent One.

Explanation: God is beyond the orbit of pain and pleasure. He bestows divine compassion and love to each created being.

89

يَا مُغْنِى

Yā Mughni

THE ENRICHER
The Bestower of Wealth,
The Sufficient.

Explanation: God gives to His created beings possessed of spotless effulgence all the good things they need and saves them from the evil things.

90

يَا مَانِعُ

yā Māni'

THE PREVENTER
The Restrainer, Withholder,
Hinderer, Prohibiter, and Forbidder.

Explanation: God, who removes the darkness of ignorance from His created beings
and bestows on them divine grace and love.

91

يَاضَآرُّ

yā Ḍarr

THE DISTRESSER
The Harmful.

Explanation: God, who on Judgment Day, causes great difficulties to satan's works, to ignorance, and to the actions emanating from ignorance.

92

يَانَافِعُ

yā Nāfiʿ

THE BENEFITER
The Advantageous,
The Profitable, The Useful.

Explanation: God, who gives good actions to
all created beings.

93

يَا نُوْرُ

yā Nūr

THE LIGHT
The Light of Completion, Perfection,
Purity, and Plenitude;
The Enlightenment; The Ray of Light.

Explanation: God gives His divine luminosity to truth, wisdom, and His divine beauty.

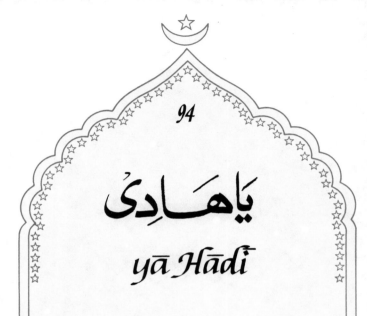

94

يَاهَادِى

yā Hādī

THE GUIDE
The Leader.

Explanation: God shows the correct path to those possessed of a spotlessly pure *qalb*.

95

يَا بَدِيعُ

yā Badiʿ

THE INCOMPARABLE
The Unprecedented;
The Extraordinary; The Originator,
Commencer, Inventor, and Creator.

Explanation: God, who creates beings of infinite variety, each more wonderful than the other, and endows each with a particular beauty.

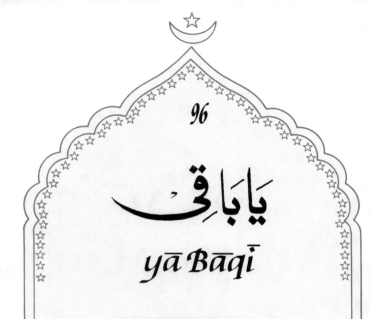

96

يَابَاقِ

yā Bāqī

THE ENDURING
The Everlasting and Eternal,
The Survivor.

Explanation: God, who never creates a thing
comparable and equal to Him.

97

يَا وَارِثُ

yā Wārith

THE INHERITOR
The Heir.

Explanation: God, who is imperishable and without end, even after the end of all created beings.

98

يَا رَشِيدُ

yā Rashīd

THE UNERRING
The Discriminating, The Director,
The Guide to the Right Path,
The Possessor of True Faith.

Explanation: God endows His created beings
with divine wisdom and, showing the path of
Īmān, enables them to merge with Him.

99

يَا صَبُوْرُ

yā ṣabūr

THE MOST PATIENT
The Long-Enduring and
Forbearant; Patience.

Explanation: God always is in a state of limit-less forbearance, compassion, patience, and justice toward each of His created beings.

Further Explanations

TURN YOUR HEART TOWARD GOD

Bismillāhirahmāniraheem: In the Name of God, the Most Merciful, the Most Gracious.

All praise and praising belong to Allah alone. He is incomparable love and limitless grace. All wealth is His by right. All wealth is His in completeness. He is the One of plenitude, the One of complete wealth.

△ This is the *qalb*, the heart; it is one fistful of earth. This heart has to be changed. It is like this now ♡ , and it must be changed to this △ . This ♡ is *Lā ilāha* [the state of many deities]. When it turns upward △ , then it becomes *ill Allāhu* [Only You are Allah!]. When the *qalb* is pointed downward, it is focused upon the 'I', the world, and creation. When it points upward, there is only God.

God will not change. He will always exist in the way that He exists. Allah is Allah. It is our heart that must be changed and turned around. The *qalb* is like this now ♡ , pointing downward like a mango. It is looking down and drooping toward the earth.

Trees, creations, all things look toward the earth and are pulled by the earth. When the mango ripens, it will fall, because it is looking at its earthly connection. The mango is staring at the earth and is eating the aspect of earth. However, if it is turned upward, God's food is there. Then it will ascend, leaving the earth and drawing its essence from Him. But now it draws it essence from the earth; it draws its essence from the differences called 'you' and 'I'. As long as we have this section, we are holding onto the earth; we have fallen down from above. We must climb up from below. My children, you *must* change your *qalb*; you must change that one handful of earth. You must change the direction of that one handful of earth toward Him.

That one handful contains solids, heat, liquids, gases, light waves, and sound waves in space [or earth, fire, water, air, and ether]. Those are the five miracles or energies [*saktis*], and they must be turned upside down and changed into angels. If you make that change, then you direct the *qalb* toward the world of the soul [*arwāh*]. It must be changed by destroying the base desires [*nafs*] and all those things it contains. It must be changed to the original mother and father, to Adam, to the soul, to

Michael, Gabriel, Israfil, and 'Izra'eel (A.S.).[3] These are the divine messengers, the heavenly messengers. Now they are solids, heat, liquids, gases, light waves, and sound waves in space. Now they have form. You must erase this form and change it into Adam, our original father, and into light. It must be made into light. That is wisdom.

Gabriel is a heavenly messenger. He brings the message of God as a revelation or *wahī*. Michael is also a messenger of the heavens. Israfil is also an angel in the heavens. There are four arch-angels [Gabriel, Michael, Israfil, and 'Izra'eel (A.S.)]. They are God's angels; they are God's heavenly messengers.

The *rūh* or soul is a ray from God. What we must do is leave this earthly form, and take on the form of the angels of God. If we are in the same form as the angels, then they will convey our intentions to God and bring God's sound back to us. These messages will be communicated through God's heavenly messenger, Gabriel. Gabriel is wisdom. God's sound or vibration is the *Qutbiyat*. The power of Allah's *Zāt* [Essence] is the *Noor* or the light of plenitude. That plenitude is God. From that plenitude radiates the light of plenitude, the *Noor*. From the *Noor* radiates His sound, the *Qutbi-*

---

[3] (A.S.) — The shortened form of *'alaihimus-salaam*: May the peace of God be upon them. A supplication traditionally spoken in Arabic after mentioning the names of prophets or archangels.

yat. The absolute power of the *Noor* radiates from the absolute power of God, and from that power of the *Noor* arises the *Qutbiyat*. From the *Qutbiyat* comes the vibration, and that sound comes to Gabriel or wisdom. Then from Gabriel it comes to Adam. (Adam is the light form of man.) This is the way that we must receive this revelation or *wahī* from Allah. We must receive the commandments of God through His messenger, Gabriel.

Children, jeweled lights in the eye of God, we need to think. Allah is not a form. He is One of great *daulat*, or treasure. Between the *sirr* [the secret of creation] and the *sifāt* [the manifestations of creation] there is the *Zāt* [the Essence]. The grace of man is the *Zāt* of God. That is the treasury of His grace; it belongs to God alone. What is known as *Zāt* is God's treasure. That treasure is *Insān*, or true man. That treasury is within the innermost heart of the true man. God's wealth is *Insān*, and *Insān*'s wealth is God. This treasury is the *Zāt*, and what originated from His *Zāt* are the secrets of His creation.

Within creation there are many kinds of wisdom, many kinds of sights, many kinds of laughter, many kinds of smells, many kinds of noses, many kinds of blood, many kinds of food, many kinds of sounds, many kinds of languages, many kinds of voices, many kinds of actions, many kinds of conduct, many kinds of intellect, many kinds of aware-

111

ness, many kinds of life, many kinds of colors and hues and methods of action. There are the creations of the seas, the creations of lands, the creations of space, the creations of the earth, the creations of fire, the creations of air, the creations of water, the creations of ether, and then there is *Insān*, man, the creation of light. Because the qualities, colors, hues, actions, and manifestations of each of these creations are varied, they are said to be His secret, the secret of God. In the flowers, in the trees, in the shrubs, in the fruits, in the food, in all those things there are differences. That is why His creation is called His secret.

What has been purified from the *sifāt* is called His *Zāt*, His grace. God has said, "This is My treasure." Because man has that *qalb*, that beauty, those qualities, that sound, that action, that speech, that analytic wisdom, that light, those explanations, that radiance, and that resplendence which understands the Father, he is called *Insān*, the son of God. He is the one who has been made pure. That is why God has said, "My secret is man, and I am his secret. I am his wealth, and he is My wealth. My story is within him, and his story is within Me. We are the son and God. He is the one who can understand this world, the world of the soul, and everything. Man will know what the angels cannot know. My prince *will* know. But there are things that even man cannot understand, things that only I will understand. I will understand all of everything. I will understand all the things which even man cannot understand.'' That is what God has said. Man is the most exalted being in all of God's creation. He is the mysterious creation of God.

God has said that what the world calls God's names are not really His names but His attributes. They are merely the duties that He performs, and they are called the *Asmā'ul-Husnā*. His qualities are His formless form. The *Asmā'ul-Husnā* is a 'printed' form. That is called the *husnā*, the beauty, man's inner form drawn of 28 letters.[4] That is the Qur'an. That beautiful form which leads to good intentions, good thoughts and a good state is the Qur'an. That is our *Guru-Ān*. [*Ān* means male in Tamil.] Allah is the only male.[5] He is our Guru. He is our Sheikh. He is our Father. He is our *Rabb* [Lord, Creator, and Protector]. He is the *Rahmān* [the Merciful One]. He is Allah. He is God. He has these qualities, and He has made this form from these qualities. His qualities exist as His form.

---

[4] The 28 letters refer to the Arabic alphabet. Each section of the human form is represented by one of these letters. When man purifies himself, these letters take the form of light and appear as the *Ummul-Qur'ān* or the eternal source of the Qur'an revealed to Muhammad (*Sal.*).

[5] Bawa defines a male as one who has no illusion within him. Thus all creations are female and in search for the One Male. God is the only One without illusion; He is the only male.

These 99 attributes are the names of His qualities.
The duties which are performed according to these
attributes are what the world calls miracles or
wilāyats.[6] What He performs is His duty, but the
world says these duties are the miracles of God.
They say they are His names, but they are not His
names. He has no name. He is a power. That Power
declares, ''There is no one who has understood Me.
There is no story for Me. No one has understood
Me. No one has found an end to Me. One who
knows Me will have died within Me; he will no
longer be outside Me. He would be dead within Me.
Therefore, there is no one who can speak of Me
knowingly. One who has understood Me does not
exist outside. One who has touched Me is not on
the outside. One who has seen Me is not on the
outside. He will not remain outside but will have
disappeared within Me. He will have gone within.
Therefore, one who sees My duties calls them My
names. That is the form of *Asmā'ul-Husnā*. Those
are My qualities, My duties, My actions, and that is
the work I do for My creations.

''That is work without selfishness; that is the
work which the Father does to protect His children,
His creations. These qualities are My form, and

[6] The *wilāyats* (commonly spelled *vilāyats*) are the miraculous
names and actions of God; the power of His attributes through
which all creations came into existence.

whoever acquires this form will be My prince. His house will be My house. His house *is* My house. His work is My work. This is the house of 28 letters. Whoever disappears within that house disappears within Me, because that is My form. That is the Qur'an. I am the Guru to one who has these qualities. I am his Guru, I am his Sheikh, I am his Father, I am his Treasure, I am his Heaven, I am his Friend, I am his Slave, I am his King. I am the One who serves him, I am a Beggar to him, I am a Rich One to him, I am his Slave, I am his Father, I am his Mother, I am the One who gives him milk, I am the One who embraces him, I am the One who carries him and who looks after him every moment.

"These qualities are My formless form. That form is the *Asmā'ul-Husnā*, My qualities, and that is the Qur'an. I have made man's form out of the 28 letters, and therefore he is called the Qur'an. Because he has all My treasures, he is the Qur'an. If he develops these qualities, he will be able to recite My Qur'an. He will read My inner Qur'an. That Qur'an is not on the outside. Man is the book. That book is within him, and he has to recite it within. He has to open himself and recite that book. He cannot recite it without opening his inner self. He has to open that Qur'an, His *qalb*. The *qalb* is made of the five Arabic letters—*alif, lām, meem, hey, dāl.* [Together these letters spell *Alhamd*—the heart of praise.] He will have to open that Qur'an. If he opens the *qalb*, he will recite everything within it. Then he will take that form of the *Asmā'ul-Husnā*, and then he will see Me. One who sees Me will merge within Me, and I will merge within him.'' This is what God has said.

Some refer to the *Asmā'ul-Husnā* as His names, but they are not His names. They are His duties, the actions of His duties which He performs. There is no name or city or place for Him. He cannot be given a name! God has said, "I am the complete and perfect One. I have no shadow, no form, no wife, no child, no associate, no beginning, and no end. I am One. I have no darkness, no torpor, no desire, no death, and no birth. I do not have any of these things. That is My state. I have no story.'' One who has no story has no name; He is only one point.

He is the Ruler of fathomless grace, the One of incomparable love. No love compares to His love. His grace has no end. That is how it is. Because of this, whenever one needs God's love, whatever his heart needs, or whatever he needs for his hunger or thirst, or for anything, his needs are satisfied through Allah's *Rahmat* [mercy, benevolence]. That is why He is called the *Rahmatul-'ālameen* [the mercy and compassion of all the universes]. He provides the wondrous blessings [*mubārakāt*] for the three worlds of *awwal, dunyā,* and *ākhir* [the beginning, this world, and the hereafter]. Whatever the soul needs; whatever the world needs, whatever creation needs; whatever the earth, fire, water, air, and ether need; whatever wisdom needs, He will give. He is the *Rahmatul-'ālameen* for the three worlds of *awwal, dunyā,* and *ākhir.* He will give the treasure which is the *mubārakāt.* The soul needs the purity of God, and He will give that. The wisdom needs the soul, and He will give that. This *Rahmat* is within Him. He says, "I have that *Rahmat,* that fathomless grace and incomparable love. Because I am the Ruler of fathomless grace, the One who is incomparable love, this is My work." He is the *Rahmatul-'ālameen.*

"Ask for whatever you need. Call Me. Ask Me." Anyone can do this, anyone in creation can do this. No matter how much is taken and taken, there is no diminishing! Take whatever is needed for your wisdom. Take whatever your hearts need. Although you take and take, there will be no diminishing from *Allāhooo*—that resonance! Because there is that one resonance, *Allāhooo,* you can take and take without any diminishing. You can take and take from that 'hoooo'. If you take some now and then take some more, the 'hoooo' will not diminish even by a drop.

Because He is the giving, giving, undiminishing treasure to your heart, He is *Allāhoooo!* Hooo, hooo, hooo, hooo, hooo, hooo, hooo, hooo is His spring, the spring water of grace. Hooo, hooo, hooo, hooo is continuously giving. You must take from it. Although you may take some, and another man may take some, and someone else may take some more, it will not diminish by even a drop. *Allāhooo* is common to all. Take! Gather the water up from the spring of *Allāhoooo!* That word is a common name given to Him. That belongs to all. It is common to all. The birds say, "Hooo...hooo... hooo...hooo." The snakes say, "Shoo...shooo... shoo." As each creation breathes, this resonance goes on. "Hooo...hooo...hoooo." Even if you close your mouth and breathe, that sound of respiration goes on. "Hooo-hoo-hoo!" If you are exhausted, that same sound of 'hooo-hoo-hoo' comes. Each one of His creations makes that sound. That sound of 'hooo' exists in everything. That 'hooo' is creation. God said the word, *"Kun!* [Be!]" to commence creation. 'Hooo' is creation calling to Him.

The treasure which has so many meanings is *Asmā'ul-Husnā,* which is the form of the qualities of God and His actions. The form of *Asmā'ul-Husnā* is *Insān,* or true man. The perfect man is *Insān Kāmil.* The form of *Insān Kāmil* will be the form of Allah. When one is called *Insān Kāmil,* the purest man, he has to have such a form. Whoever has that form has the form of God, the house of God. That is God's form. Once the form of God's qualities develops within a man, that man merges within God. His speech, his sight, his sense of smell, his sound, his *qalb,* and his body disappear within God. Then

118

all sounds that come from him will be sounds that come from God. But if those sounds come from what is known as the 'I', or the ego, then he is not in that form but in the form of satan.

When Gabriel came to explain the *Asmā'ul-Husnā* (the qualities of God) and to bring the revelations to the prophets, he also spoke of the actions of God... God is like this, God does this, and God does that. These revelations were given lastly to Muhammad (*Sal.*). Muhammad (*Sal.*) is the final prophet. Gabriel gave him these 99 explanations, but God has 3,000 gracious qualities. Through Gabriel, God also explained how He had distributed His 3,000 gracious qualities. "My blessings exist in many ways. O Muhammad, My blessings exist in many ways. There will be no prophets after you. You are the last prophet. You have the pearl of the plenitude of grace. Therefore, I am going to explain to you this pearl's 3,000 gracious qualities." He sent this message through Gabriel.

He said to Muhammad (*Sal.*), "There are many kinds of beings amongst My creations. In My creation there are many beings existing in various sections with various qualities. To the angels, the heavenly beings, the celestial beings, to the heavenly lights, and to the heavenly beings in space, the sun, and the moon, I have given 1,000 of the 3,000 qualities. I have given 1,000 gracious qualities to protect these heavenly beings. I have given another

1,000 of My gracious qualities to My representatives, My prophets, My saints, and My *qutbs*.

"Because My creations are of many kinds and their qualities are many, because they have the quality of living by killing and eating one another, I have given 300 of these gracious qualities to the *Zaboor* religion, the Hindu group of religions which relates to creation. These 300 qualities were given to this first stage, the stage of creation, for the sake of developing patience, tolerance, and compassion.

"Secondly, there are the *Hānal* religions which worship fire. Fire is light, noise, hunger, anger, and murder. Because fire does not know good and bad, it will burn and devour anything. If hunger attacks someone, the Ten Commandments fly away. If there is an ailment, even to one of their own kin, people will reject him. If old age comes to their father, they will reject him, saying, 'What is the use of this old man? Let him die.' To make them understand all this, I have given 300 of My gracious qualities. I am not giving My duties to them, but I am only giving My qualities. They cannot be given My duties. They cannot perform My duty. Out of My gracious qualities, I am giving 300 to the *Hānal* religions.

"Then comes the third stage, *Injeel,* the Christian group of religions, to which I have also given 300 of My gracious qualities. I have made this secret body out of millions and millions of kinds of gases. From My letter *alif* (**ا**), I have taken a *sukoon* (◦) and then a *nuqat* (•),[7] a dot from which I have created these 18,000 universes and all creations. The creations of the ocean, creations of the land and earth, creations of heaven and hell, the jinns, the fairies, the angels, satan, birds, and reptiles—all these creations and the 18,000 universes have been made into a *sukoon*. I made them all a *nuqat* within a *nuqat*, a dot within a dot. I made all of the worlds into a *nuqat*, a dot, and placed it within the *qalb* of man. Within that *qalb*, I made the essence and forms of all creations into a shadow. Then I made that into a particle, and within that particle, I placed My secret. Within the secret within that secret, I placed gases, vibrations, all spiritual things, all the universes, and all the miracles. I made a particle of a particle within that secret into wisdom. I then made that wisdom within wisdom to be the *Noor*. That is My *Zāt*, and from My *Zāt*, I made everything. Within everything is My secret. I made that as a mystery.

"That mystery is the basis of the faith of Islam, and I have made that into *Insān*. I have made that mystery as the fourth stage, as *Furqān*, as Islam.

---

[7] A *sukoon* is an Arabic diacritical mark in the shape of an open circle. A *nuqat* is also a diacritical mark, but written as a solid dot. Although *nuqat* (dots) is the plural form of *nuqtah* or dot, it arbitrarily will be used in the text for both singular and plural to avoid confusion.

Within that mystery, I made the sight, the smell, sound, speech, and *qalb* into a flower. Within that flower, I placed My complete beauty of the wealth of the wondrous blessing. I made the beauty of My attributes as nourishment [*rizq*]. I exist as the taste within that nourishment. Within that taste, I made the never-ending light of plenitude which can see the world, the hereafter, and everything. I made that into My kingdom. That is My kingdom. Within that kingdom, I have placed everything that is to be seen. That is My *Zāt*. I have made that into *Insān*, and within *Insān*, I have made My 99 qualities, My duties, into *Furqān*. I have made *Insān* into the *Asmā'ul-Husnā*, and I manifested My qualities within the form of the *Asmā'ul-Husnā*. These are My duties. The actions of these qualities are My duty. Within the *Asmā'ul-Husnā*, within the *sūrat* [form] known as *Insān* are My qualities. These are My duties, and this is My prince.

"Of all My qualities, one remains in My hand and that is an undiminishing treasure. One out of the 3,000 qualities exists in My hand. If one understands My qualities which are the form of the *Asmā'ul-Husnā* and acts with these qualities, then he is My prince. But that one power remains in My hand. That power, *Allāhu,* is in My hand. But one who establishes this state of *Asmā'ul-Husnā* will be My prince. He will be Me. These 99 are the duties of My qualities. These are the 99 powers. These 99 together with the one pure power is My complete power. That one power is always in My hand. That power of creating, making, destroying, nourishing, and sustaining is with Me. No one else will be able to do these duties. Without this one power, nothing would be fed and nothing would move. Without this power, nothing happens. Even an atom will not move. Even an atom needs this power. What comprises this state of *Asmā'ul-Husnā* are My gracious qualities and My actions. It is these actions, these duties which are the *Asmā'ul-Husnā*. That is the *Asmā'ul-Husnā*. Those are My duties.

"O Muhammad, I have given the meanings of these 3,000 qualities and My duty to My prophets. I have taught them as commandments to the prophets. I have given them to the 124,000 prophets. Of these 124,000 prophets, I have made 25 prophets most clear. Of the 25, I have made eight even more clear. They are Adam, Noah, Abraham, Isma'il, David, Moses, Jesus, and Muhammad. These eight prophets exist as the eight heavens. I will give the appropriate heaven to whomever accepts one of these eight sections. These eight actions of mine will be given to whomever establishes their particular state. Each will be given his own place. O Muhammad, I have established this state. I will explain to you all the gracious qualities and everything that I have revealed to My prophets. What I have told to My earlier prophets, I will now tell you.

I have told them to perform My duty, My actions. 'Do this. Do this. Do this.' In these 6,666 verses,[8] I will reveal to you again these commandments which have been given before.''

Then God revealed to Muhammad (*Sal.*) these 6,666 verses. What He had revealed to the earlier prophets, God revealed again to the last prophet, Muhammad (*Sal.*). Gabriel conveyed these *wahīs* or revelations to Allah's Prophet (*Sal.*). These revelations are called the Qur'an. They are called the Triple Qur'an [Tamil: *Tiru Marai*]. It is called the *Tiru Marai* or the *Tiru Qur'ān. Tiru* means three: *awwal, dunyā,* and *ākhir*—the world of the souls, this world of form, and the world of the hereafter. These three worlds are hidden within that *Tiru Qur'ān.* Further, the state of *anāthi* [the beginning-less beginning], *āthi* [the resplendent time of grace], and everything connected to God which has been hidden is within the *Tiru Marai* or the *Tiru Qur'ān.* Every created thing, the earth, the skies, the nether worlds, the earth, fire, water, air, and ether exist in the *Tiru Marai* without self-image, without form, without body, without shadow. God created and concealed them within the *Tiru Qur'ān* or the *Tiru Marai.* The wisdom which exists as the

8 6,666 refers to the number of *āyats* (verses or signs) in the Qur'an. According to various traditions and methods of recital this is reckoned between 6,204 and 6,239. However, according to certain Sufi traditions they number 6,666.

teacher and which leads us on the path is the *Tiru Qur'ān*. "It is this *Tiru Qur'ān* that I am giving you, O Muhammad," God said. "This contains all that I told My earlier prophets. But to you I will give everything in completeness. May you explain this to your children, to your followers!"

This is the explanation that Gabriel brought to Muhammad (*Sal.*). Gabriel said, "Allah bid me to say this to you." That is what is called the Qur'an. If one understands the meaning of this Qur'an, he will understand the duty of Allah and the compassionate qualities of Allah. If he accepts these qualities and becomes this form, then he will understand the Qur'an, then he will understand his Father, and he will know there is only one family and one God. Until then, he will never understand the Qur'an. One family and one God—that is what he will understand. Then he has nothing else—no fighting, no differences, no quarrels. None of these things will exist. Allah gave this explanation so that we might understand.

These explanations are a direct vibration from Allah. Muhammad (*Sal.*) received the vibrations directly. But what people have seen is not Muhammad (*Sal.*). What they have written about is not Muhammad (*Sal.*). He is not the form they have seen. The true histories of Moses, Jesus, and Muhammad (*Sal.*) are not the way people have seen it, or heard it, or spoken of it, or written about it. What

125

they saw is really different from the truth. At one time, Muhammad (*Sal.*) said, ''I have not spoken one word other than the word of Allah. Without His commandment, without His word, I would not have said anything. Everything that comes from me comes from Him, not me.''

The people of that time had a huge mountain of Sinai in their hearts. That is the mountain where satan and illusion live. Breaking that mountain of illusion within them was very difficult. Moses came earlier under these same circumstances, and his followers gave him an indescribable amount of agony. Those same people made Muhammad (*Sal.*), who was the final prophet, undergo many difficulties. It is very difficult to shatter the hard rock of jealousy known as Mt. Sinai, the mountain of the seven desires of illusion which extends up to the skies. It is very difficult to shatter this ego rock known as the 'I', this rock which cannot be broken. To break that away from the people of that time, to break them away from the family of satan, and to break them away from their pagan religions was very difficult.

There were a few who followed the Prophet (*Sal.*); if they had not followed him, they would have killed much more than they did. Some words had to be given gradually, and some words had to be clarified further after a little while. Otherwise, the people would have murdered much more than they did. Many things like this happened to Muhammad (*Sal.*) and the other prophets. They had to undergo much agony and difficulty to stop these murders and these sins. The *qurbān* [the commandment of saying the Third *Kalimah* when ritually slaughtering animals] was also sent down to stop this murdering. And like this, the difference between *haraam* [not permissible] and *halaal* [permissible] was sent down. All the prophets came in order to gradually correct the people, to gradually reduce the number of murders, to gradually reduce theft, to reduce what is *haraam*, to reduce the actions against God's commandments, to gradually reduce the sacrifices, and to gradually reduce arrogance. Gradually, little by little by little, these were lessened.

A *HADĪSZ QUDSĪ* [9]

Muhammad (*Sal.*) spoke only according to the commandment of God. Muhammad (*Sal.*) said, "Without the commandments, without Allah's permission, I would not have spoken one word."

One day, Gabriel had the thought, "I brought these 6,666 verses to Muhammad. I brought the messages to each prophet. I was the messenger for each of them. I brought the commandments to all of

---

[9] A *Hadīsz Qudsī* is a direct communication between the Prophet (*Sal.*) and Allah without the medium of the Angel Gabriel.

the prophets.'' That was the idea which came to Gabriel.

Allah knew his thoughts. So, God summoned Gabriel and said, ''Go! Give Muhammad My *salaams* and give him this verse to recite. Tell him to say, '*Saboor* [patience and tolerance].' Tell him to give this to his followers.''

But when that word came forth, the one who brought it, brought the 'I'. He brought the arrogance. What is known as the 'I' came to Gabriel. He came with the thought, ''I am the one who gave so much to Muhammad.'' He was supposed to bring *saboor* as Allah had said, but what Gabriel had was the 'I'. ''I, myself, am bringing this,'' he thought. He addressed Muhammad (*Sal.*), ''As-salaamu 'alaikum, O Muhammad.''

Then the Prophet (*Sal.*) said, '''*Alaikumus-salaam*.''

And Gabriel said, ''Allah sends His *salaams* to you.''

''Allah? Who are you?'' asked Muhammad (*Sal.*). ''Who are you?''

Then Gabriel said, ''O Muhammad, do you not know me? I am Gabriel!''

''Is that so? I have never seen you before.''

''You do not know me? I am the one who brought all the *āyats* [verses or signs of God] to you and to the other prophets!''

Then Muhammad (*Sal.*) said, ''I have never

seen you before. I have not seen you at all.''

Gabriel said, ''Allah told me to say this to you.''

''Did He? Have you seen Allah?'' asked Muhammad (*Sal.*).

''No. I have not seen Allah.''

''Then if you have not seen Allah, how can you tell me what Allah has said? How can I accept it? I have not seen you before, and I do not accept the word which you bring now. I will not accept the word of one who has not seen Allah. You have not seen Allah, and I have never seen you before.''

Gabriel was shocked. ''You have not seen me earlier? But I brought you so much!''

''No, I have not seen you.''

''But I am Gabriel!''

''I have not seen you. I do not accept you. You have not seen Allah, and I have never seen you before. You have not seen Allah, so how can you know Allah's words? How can I accept what you say?''

Gabriel went back and complained to Allah. ''Allah! Muhammad said that he has not seen me before. I brought him *saboor*, Your patience, but he did not accept it. He asked me if I had seen Allah, and I said that I had not seen You. He said that he had never seen me before, and that he could not accept the word of one who has not seen God.'' Gabriel then asked, ''Allah! What shall I do now?''

God said, "Gabriel, look at the world of the soul [*arwāh*]." Then the world of the soul opened, and 70,000 veils were opened. He looked beyond the 70,000 veils, and an indescribable veil was there. Its description has no limit. All divine rays radiated from that veil, and a second veil was behind it. Green lights were emanating and radiating from it. None of those rays of light could be described. The powerful light of each piercing ray penetrated from this world to the world of the soul. Then the second veil opened. The third veil was emerald green with pulsating light-beams, spreading coolness everywhere. Then the third veil opened, and a round brilliance was there. It is impossible to speak about that light. The *Noor! Noor Muhammad!* was written there. From it came a vibration, a sound. A sound came. A sound came from that light.

"Go say this! Go say this! Go tell this to Muhammad!" That was the sound, *Noor Muhammad!* When Gabriel looked, there was the face of a sixteen-year-old youth in a light-form with a very small moustache.

Gabriel asked, "Who are you?"

"Hi! *Hayy!*" He said. (*'Hayy'* is an Arabic word. *'Yā'* and *'Hayy'* are wondrous words. *'Yā'* is praise, and *'Hayy'* is praise. They are secret words. *'Yā'* means praise. Among some of the words of Allah, *'Hayy!'* and *'Yā!'* are secret words.)

Then Allah asked, "Did you see who that was? Gabriel, do you see who it is? I am the *Noor*. The *Noor* is I. They are not two. Allah, Muhammad. Muhammad, Allah. This form is the *Zāt*, the grace. It is within Me, and I am within It. It is that completeness which is emitting sound. I do not speak; it speaks. I exist within it, and it exists within Me. It speaks My word, and I speak its word. I explain things to My creation through this light. The One who is there and the One who is here are One.

"There are three *meems*.[10] I am the light *meem*. That is the *Noor meem*. That is My beautiful *meem*, the form which has come to My creation. I have revealed Muhammad so that the people will believe. I made this form and this beauty and veiled it with seven robes. This is what is being shown to you now, and this is what exists within. That is what is within the seven robes. That is Muhammad. Muhammad is My beauty, My face, My *qalb*, My grace, My *Zāt*. That is what Muhammad is.

"For this reason, I have made you carry the revelations as a witness. Because I do not give form

[10] The three *meems* (the Arabic letter م) refer to the mystical nature of Muhammad (*Sal.*). They are: the Light (*Noor*) *meem*, the physical form which came from the spermatazoa shaped like a *meem*, and the *meem* of the resplendent soul. The *meem* of the soul represents the beginning (*awwal*), the *meem* of the form represents the world (*dunyā*), and the *meem* of the *Noor* represents the hereafter (*ākhir*).

131

to what is formless, I created you to speak as a witness to provide the proof. But what did you say when you left the last time? When you were going, Gabriel, you said, 'I, myself, taught the 124,000 prophets. And I, myself, am preaching to Muhammad now. I, myself, am the guru. Without me, how could God tell Muhammad anything? I am older than Muhammad. I do it all. Allah gives it to me to tell, and I myself am the one who says it.' Did you not think like that? You were thinking that as you were going. You were going along thinking, 'I'. The place where the 'I' exists is satan's domain. Then you are not Gabriel. That is why Muhammad (*Sal.*) did not accept you.

If you had understood where the revelation came from, who it came from, who it was going to, who is the one listening, who is the one bringing it, and who is the one speaking it, then you could have understood the *saboor* which you were bringing. Because you did not understand *saboor*, because you went to Muhammad bringing the 'I', he did not accept you." Then God said, "Go. Now tell him this. But first you must understand *saboor*."

Then Gabriel said, "We will go. I will not do that any more. Allah will give the message."

He went to Muhammad (*Sal.*) and said, "*Assalaamu 'alaikum, Rasoolullāh,* O Prophet of Allah."

"'*Alaikumus-salaam,* Gabriel. Have you come

132

only now?''

"I came before."

"Oh. I did not see you then. I saw you only now. There was someone who resembled you but came in the form of a satan. He said he brought the word known as *saboor*. He said, 'Allah said this.' But I saw satan then, and he had no *saboor*. That is why I told him to go. Now you have come as the real Gabriel. Now I see you. You are the one who brought the revelations before. Now I see you, and now I accept you. Have you seen Allah yet?'' He embraced him.

"Yes...yes...I saw Him...in a way. This is what I saw. This is what I saw,'' said Gabriel. He explained all that happened and he embraced Muhammad (*Sal.*).

Then Muhammad (*Sal.*) told Gabriel, "You must accept *saboor* within yourself and then give *saboor* to me. Then the 'I' will not exist.'' That is what he taught Gabriel.

There are secret graces which exist like this. When a revelation is being received from Allah, we must exist as Allah. What exists within Allah goes to Allah. Muhammad (*Sal.*) speaks Allah's commandments from within Allah. Allah exists within Muhammad (*Sal.*), speaking His commandments. It is like this that we, existing within Allah, must speak of Allah's commandments. Allah, existing within us, must speak Allah's commandments.

133

Until the time that this state is understood, the commandments of Allah will not be heard.

Muhammad (*Sal.*) said, "There are things Allah has told me in addition to the *āyats* that were brought. I will never speak words that Allah has not spoken!" Some words were revealed which came directly to the *qalb*. They were words which Gabriel could never conceive of; words so heavy with grace! Gabriel could not have borne the weight. He could not have carried them. Words that Gabriel could not carry came straight to Muhammad (*Sal.*). They were very heavy.

"Try to carry this. Try to carry this," said God, but Gabriel could not carry them. He could not carry them. Allah said, "This is the grace, the *Zāt!*" When this heavy thing is given, it is given directly. It is His *Rahmat* which gives the explanation.

If the children's intention is upon Allah, this is how they speak to Him in their *qalbs*. God has taught this state to Muhammad (*Sal.*), and you must establish this state. You must make this physical form into that form. If you establish that state and that duty then you can receive His *daulat*, the true wealth.

According to a *Hadīsz Qudsī*, God has said, "O Muhammad, without you I would not have created anything."

Who are we? We must understand who we are. God's *qalb*, His heart, is the *Zāt*, the grace. The

134

heart [*aham* in Tamil] and the face [*muham* in Tamil] are the beauty of Allah-Muhammad! The *qalb* and the face. The *qalb* is Allah's treasury. The face is Allah's beauty. The two merged as one is Muhammad (*Sal.*). Without these two, God would not have made anything into form. He would not have created anything without *Zāt*, without His beauty, His light. Nothing would have been created. That is why Allah has said, ''O Muhammad, I have not created anything without you.'' His *Zāt* is the heart (*aham*)! That is grace! His beauty! Light!

''Without these two, I would not have created anything. My beauty and grace are necessary! My grace and My beauty are necessary! O Muhammad, I would not have created anything without you. Without this beauty and grace, I would not have made anything. You are the treasure which has manifested from Me. You are the beauty revealed from within Me.'' Muhammad (*Sal.*) is His beauty, the beauty of the heart, the secret of the *qalb*, the *Zāt* that is grace.

''Both are revealed from within Me. I would never have created anything without them. Because you have been revealed from within Me as My face (*muham*) and My heart (*aham*), I will create everything with you.'' Allah has said this.

Who are we? That heart and that face are the light form. That is Muhammad (*Sal.*). That face (*muham*) and that heart (*aham*) is His form. That must exist within. That must speak with Allah. That form must speak; that beauty and that *qalb* must speak. God within that beauty and you within Him — that is the name known as Muhammad (*Sal.*). What is its end? When did it begin? When was it manifested? When will it disappear? We cannot calculate its time.

Many names have been given to the Prophet Muhammad (*Sal.*), but there are eleven which are the causal names, the explanatory names derived from His state, names bestowed upon Muhammad by Allah at the time when he was within Allah and was being manifested. All the other names were given later, after Muhammad's manifestation; they are his *wilāyats*. These names were bestowed in *arwāh* when Muhammad was the resplendence of Allah. This resplendence exists within every man and can be seen as that beauty, if one looks within.

The Eleven Names of Muhammad

1. *Anāthi Muhammad*
   The Unmanifested

2. *Āthi Muhammad*
   The Manifested

3. *Awwal Muhammad*
   The Beginning, the emergence of creation

136

4. *Hayāt Muhammad*
   The *Rūh*, the emergence of the soul

5. *An'am Muhammad*
   The Food, the *Rizq* or nourishment for all creations

6. *Ahmad*
   The Heart, the *Qalb*

7. *Muhammad*
   The Beauty of the face which is a reflection of the Beauty of the heart

8. *Noor Muhammad*
   The Plenitude, the Light which became completeness within Allah and emerged

9. *Allāh-Muhammad*
   The Light of Allah within Muhammad, and the Light of Muhammad within Allah

10. *Rathina Muhammad*
    The above nine are combined into one, and that is the Jewel Muhammad, the Muhammad of the Nine Precious Gems

11. *Karanam Muhammad*
    The Causal Muhammad, the Cause for all creation and for all of history

ANOTHER *HADĪSZ QUDSĪ*

One day Gabriel was told to bring a *wahī*, a revelation to Muhammad (*Sal.*). Allah said, ''Please give Muhammad My *salaam*. Please give him My love.'' God said this and then revealed a new verse of the Qur'an [*āyat*] to Gabriel.

Gabriel brought this to Muhammad (*Sal.*), but the Prophet had already gone out. Fatimah (*Ral.*), [11] Muhammad's daughter, was at the doorstep when Gabriel came. ''*As-salaamu 'alaikum,*'' said Fatimah (*Ral.*).

''Fatimah, where is the Prophet?''

''He has gone out. *As-salaamu 'alaikum.* Please come in, O my uncle, younger brother of my father. Please sit down.''

Gabriel got a little angry. He stood there without saying anything. A little while went by, and he still would not sit down. He just stood there. Fatimah (*Ral.*) said, ''O younger brother of my father, what I said (*As-salaamu 'alaikum*) is the praise of God. I spoke the *Rahmat* and the praise of God. You did not give the reply. I am not angry, but you did not return my *salaam.* It is your responsibility. By this omission you have incurred a great debt. You did not reply to the *salaam*, to Allah's word,

---

[11] Here (*Ral.*) is the shortened form of *Radhiyallāhu 'anhā,* the feminine form of the supplication said after mentioning the name of a saint. ''May Allah be pleased with her.''

and that is a debt which you owe. A serious debt.

Gabriel immediately replied, "*Alaikumus-salaam, 'alaikumus-salaam*, Fatimah."

Why were you angry with me?"

"It has nothing to do with you. But your father is not very old. He is 50 or 52 years old. How old I am! I have brought revelations to so many prophets from Allah. I brought them to the 124,000 prophets. But you called me the younger brother of your father. That is what I was thinking about. You called me the younger brother of your father. That is what I was thinking about while I stood without speaking."

"Is that the way it is? All right. I do not know about this matter," said Fatimah (*Ral.*). Allah was smashing Gabriel's arrogance. Allah made Fatimah (*Ral.*) speak like that. He made these words within her. "Is that the way it is? I do not know anyone's age, who is bigger and who is smaller. I do not know if this one is bigger or if that one is bigger. Therefore, let my father come. I want to know which of you is older."

"All right."

The Prophet (*Sal.*) came in a little while. "*Assalaamu 'alaikum*. Gabriel, please come. Please come and sit down."

"Allah gives you His *salaam*. Allah said to give you His *salaam*."

"All right. Please sit down."

As he was seating himself, Fatimah (*Ral.*) spoke. "Father, there has been a small dispute between the two of us, between my uncle, your younger brother, and me. A mind-fight. It is disturbing both of us. I need to know which of the two of you is older. Who is older and who is younger?"

"What happened?" he asked.

Then she said, "Gabriel, may peace be upon him, came. He asked for you, but you had gone out. I said, '*As-salaamu 'alaikum*, please come in, younger brother of my father.' But he got angry. Then after a little while, when he did not reply, I said, 'This will be a debt that you will owe.' Then he replied to the *salaam*, and I asked him why he was behaving like that. He said, 'I am very old and you call me the younger brother of your father. I am much older than your father.' Therefore, which of the two of you is older? I must know the answer."

"All right then. Was it so, Gabriel?" asked the Prophet (*Sal.*). "Since you say you are older than I, what is the greatest thing in the world? Have you ever seen a wonder before I came?"

"Yes. I *have* seen a wonder in the world."

"Have you? What is the wonder?"

"There is a star which shines in the northwest. The moon is there. That star remains visible for 70,000 years, then it disappears for the next 70,000 years, but then rises again for another 70,000 years. I have seen the rising of this star 70,000 times. I have seen it."

"Have you? Do you see the star now?"

"I do not see it now."

"If you were to see it, would you recognize it in order to say whether or not it was one you had seen before? Would you be able to say if you had or had not seen it?"

"Yes. I could. I could."

Then the Rasool (*Sal.*) took off his turban. He took off the turban which exists as the *mubārakāt* [wondrous blessings] of the *'Arsh* [the throne of God]. He took off the turban which was the *mubārakat*, the treasure of Allah's *'Arsh*. He took off the crown, where the *Rahmat* for the three worlds exists, and he showed Gabriel the top of his head. That star was there, radiating. Gabriel saw it, embraced him, and started crying. He cried.

"Why are you crying? Do not cry. What are you crying about? Is this perhaps the star?"

"It is. It is. This is the star."

"Oh, really?"

Gabriel cried on and on.

"Why are you crying?"

"This is the star that I saw. But there were three symbols on that star. The symbols are not here now, just the star."

"What symbols?"

"On the head of the star was a turban. Around the neck of the star was a necklace of pendant emeralds. On the two ears of that star were two earrings. I do not see them now.''

Then Muhammad (*Sal.*) explained, ''The turban or crown of Allah's *Dhahūt*, of Allah's throne, which is known as *Dars ul-Ambiyā'*, is Allah's justice. *Dars ul-Ambiyā'* [lit. the Teachings of the Prophets] is 'Ali, the tiger of Allah's *'Arsh*, of Allah's throne.''[12] The *Dars ul-Ambiyā'* is the tiger of the *'Arsh*, His crown, the crown of His justice, the throne on which He is seated. That is the power of *Īmān* [absolute faith, certitude, and determination] which pierces and stops anything this world brings. That power is His *Dhahūt*. That is the *Īmān* of pure determination and certitude which can overcome anything illusion brings. That is called *Hadhrat 'Alī.*[13]

''The necklace of emeralds is Fatimah who said, 'Please come, younger brother of my father.' That is the girl who invited you in. The jeweled earrings are *Hasan* and *Husain.*[14] The meanings are different. There are meanings and meanings for

[12] 'Ali (*Ral.*) was one of the first to accept that Muhammad (*Sal.*) was a prophet and became the son-in-law of Muhammad (*Sal.*). He is known in Arabic as *Asadullāh*, the ''Lion of God.''

[13] *Hadhrat* is a respectful form of address for one who is in the state of being in the presence of God.

[14] Hasan and Husain are the sons of 'Ali (*Ral.*) and Fatimah (*Ral.*), the daughter of Muhammad (*Sal.*).

this. This is that star. Do you understand?''

Only Allah understands the secret of 'Ali. God alone understands the meaning, the treasure known as Fatimah. Of the two earrings, one is the *sifāt*, and one is the *Zāt*. Allah has said, ''What appeared from within Me as creation is *sifāt*, and what appeared from within Me as the light of explanation is the *Zāt*.'' These are two earrings. One earring is creation. The other earring is the *Zāt* or grace. The necklace of emeralds is Allah's beauty.

There are nine kinds of gems. There are nine openings—two eyes, two nostrils, two ears, one mouth, and two below. This is the form known as *Fātihah*. That is the energy of this world. '*Partiyā*' means, 'Did you look at the form?' *Sūratul-Fātihah*.[15] ''There is another form within this form. That is the star you saw. The beauty of Allah. The adornment. The adornment of that light. That is His beauty. That is what you saw.

'''Ali is Allah's justice. That is a tiger! It overcomes all evil qualities. He overcomes everything without any fear at all. He is the one who can hold

---

[15] '*Partiyā*' is a Tamil word meaning, ''Have you looked?'' The Arabic word, '*Sūratul-Fātihah*' is the opening chapter of the Qur'an. However, *sūrat* spelled with a different Arabic 's' also means 'form' or 'body'. Noting this, Bawa sometimes refers to the *Sūratul-Fātihah* as 'the Inner Form of Man'. And by punning with the word '*partiyā*', he is asking, ''Have you seen this inner form?''

the throne of God. He is the tiger of the *'Arsh*, the throne upon which Allah is seated. He never fails in justice. These are the adornments and the star. Now do you see? Who is older?'' asked Muhammad (*Sal.*).

"Allah alone will know you," said Gabriel, bowing his head.

Like this, the soul, the heart (*aham*) and the face (*muham*) of man have not appeared just now. Those qualities, that *qalb*, and that beauty are Allah's. When did Allah appear? When these appeared within Him, that is Muhammad (*Sal.*). *Ahmad*. His age has to be explained in the way it was told to Gabriel. That is the star, the *Noor*, the light which comes from God. That is the light. *Insān* is what that power is called. It has no end. It has no age. No matter which angel comes to ask about it, he will find that secret to be the secret of *Insān*. That is Muhammad (*Sal.*) of the *Noor*. That is the *Zāt*. It has such enormous power.

Anything that has appeared, whether it be angels, or anything else, the heavenly beings, Gabriel or Michael—God created all of these things with this beauty, that heart [*aham*], and that essence [*Zāt*]. With this grace, He has created the oceans, the lands, the world, the nether worlds, the sun, the moon, the stars—everything—heaven and hell, all the angels, heavenly beings, jinns, fairies, and everything. It is only from this light that all

144

things are created; they were not created from themselves. Creations have an estimate, but this has no estimate. Its age cannot be estimated. This has been manifested from His state, and therefore, this explanation was given to Gabriel.

This is Muhammad (*Sal.*). *Ahmad*. The *aham* (heart) and the *muham* (face) came from Allah. The *Zāt*, the grace, and the beauty came from Allah. That is what is given the name Muhammad (*Sal.*). This is not something that can be recited in an ordinary way. This is what must speak with Him. This is what *does* speak with Him. This is what reaches Him. The son of God is what returns to merge with what it came from. The son of God is what again reaches the place from which it was revealed. It is like this in the Qur'an.

We must understand the duties and the meanings of the *Asmā'ul-Husnā*. We must understand His duty. The *Asmā'ul-Husnā* is the performance of Allah's duty, the duty of His compassionate qualities, the duty which He performs for His creation. The world says that the *Asmā'ul-Husnā* are His *wilāyats*, His miracles. What is duty to Allah is a miracle to the world. This is the *Asmā'ul-Husnā*. This is the duty which we have to do. We must do the work of Allah's compassionate qualities. Taking the form of Allah's qualities and doing Allah's duty is the Qur'an. Everything else must be sacrificed.

Cut away everything else with, "*Subhān Allāhi*

145

walhamdu lillāhi wa lā ilāha ill Allāhu wallāhu akbar wa lā hawla wa lā quwwata illā billāhi wa huwal 'alīyul-'alheem.'' [16] Sacrifice everything else. Having sacrificed, having performed the *qurbān* on everything else, what remains beyond is the Qur'an. *Qurbān* is not slaughtering chickens and cows and goats. There are four hundred trillion, ten thousand beasts here in the heart which must be slaughtered. They must be slaughtered in the *qalb*. After these things have been slaughtered, what is eaten can then be distinguished as either *halaal* [permissible] or *haraam* [forbidden]. Everything that is seen in the world is *haraam*. What is seen in Allah alone is *halaal*. Please eat that.

There will be a difference in the meaning between what I say and the way you recite the Qur'an. Recite it, but find a sheikh who is an *Insān Kāmil* [a true man] and listen to him. The others do not understand. This needs to be learned from a sheikh.

What is Allah's is not secret [*sirr*]. What is secret did not come to Muhammad (*Sal.*). There is

[16] "All glory is God's and all praise is God's, and none is God except Allah and Allah is most great. And there is no majesty or power except in God, and He is the exalted, the supreme!"

This Third *Kalimah* was revealed and explained to Prophet Muhammad (*Sal.*) for the purpose of removing the beastly qualities of the animals about to be slaughtered for food and for the purpose of destroying the beastly animals within the heart of man. See Appendix for further explanation.

146

one power and one alone which He kept as secret. He has given everything else. He said, "Muhammad, say this!" It is not right to call everything secret just because we do not understand, saying, "This is secret. It cannot be revealed." They do not know! Why would He have told Muhammad (*Sal.*) what was secret? Gabriel knows it, Muhammad (*Sal.*) knows it, and Muhammad's (*Sal.*) followers know it. That is not *sirr*. It has been revealed. There is one secret, and it belongs to Allah. The secret is that He is the Endless One. The secret is that He is the Fathomless One, the Endless One. He holds that within His hand. Everything else has been revealed. Yes, it has all been told. We must understand this.

THE OCEAN OF DIVINE KNOWLEDGE

The *Asmā'ul-Husnā* is the wealth [*daulat*] of Allah, the power of Allah, the actions of Allah, the conduct of Allah, the virtuous qualities of Allah, and the virtuous behavior of Allah. It is His grace and His total wealth, including His *Zāt* [Essence] and *sifāts* [manifestations], *sharr* [evil] and *khair* [good], hell and heaven, good actions and bad actions, the day of questioning in the grave, and the day of judgment, *dunyā* [this world], and *ākhir* [next world]. The totality of everything is condensed and brought into action within the duties [*wilāyats*] of Allah. That is called the *Asmā'ul-Husnā*.

147

The *Asmā'ul-Husnā* is a vast ocean of Divine Knowledge, the *Bahrul-'Ilm*. That is the ocean of grace and wisdom. It is not something we can hope to understand with the learning that we have acquired and stored within ourselves. As long as the *qalb* is kept turned downwards, towards the section of creation, then it will see only the secrets [*sirr*] and the manifestations [*sifāts*] of Allah in the 18,000 universes. These manifestations are all examples. They are the things that can be seen on the outside as scenes. Painting pictures of these creations, writing and researching about these things, is merely the study of examples.

What do we mean by examples? Being a manifestation [*sifāt*] of Allah, every man is an example, every creation in the world is an example. Every creation contains the 15 worlds and also the 18,000 universes, but only man can know and understand these many realms. Man dwells in the ether as well as on the earth. The jinns, the fairies, the angels, and the deities do exist even though they are not visible; the birds and the animals also exist, each of these dwelling in their respective stations. But no matter what station they dwell in, they are all connected to creation, whether they be in the skies or in the earth. Creation is this circle that goes round and round. We must think about this.

Divine Knowledge or *'Ilm*, on the other hand, is to discover what is contained within these manifestations. To do this, man's *qalb* must be directed upward. It must give up whatever it saw and enjoyed and learned when it was directed downward, and must look up to the path that leads toward Allah. The *qalb* must look upward in order to see Him, to watch His actions, to see only Him. But the section of the elements (earth, fire, water, and air) only wanders below and looks about the earth or roams the ether. Both the ether and the earth have these same components. This is why, even if someone can fly in the sky, his eyes remain directed toward the earth; and if he is looking toward the earth, then his *qalb* remains focused on the manifestations of creation, the *sifāts*. That is not *'Ilm*.

'Ilm, or Divine Knowledge, is a vast ocean [*Bahr*]. That *'Ilm* exists as a mystery. It exists in the three worlds: the world of the soul [*awwal*]; the world of creations [*dunyā*]; and the world of resplendent light, the world of complete perfection, the kingdom of God [*ākhir*]. *'Ilm* understands all that fills these three worlds in completeness. *'Ilm* is that which understand the grace or *Rahmat* of all three worlds. To learn and acquire this *'Ilm*, the Rasool has said, "Search for knowledge even if you have to go unto China." We must realize what this means.

If there is a *fathah* over *alif* [ ] and a *sukoon* over *lām* [ ], we have to connect the two sounds together. The *sukoon* is this world. In the same way that we add the diacritical marks to make a sound out of letters that would otherwise be silent, the *qalb* of man needs to be connected to that *fathah* of *'Ilm*, thus producing the sound of God.[17] It is only when we make this connection, that this creation called the world is annihilated from within us. Then the *qalb* which was directed down towards creation now begins to look upwards towards Allah.

The *Asmā'ul-Husnā* are the 99 *wilāyats* of Allah. We must focus within to know the meaning. *Asmā'ul-Husnā—husnā* [the beauty] is that which is permanent, and *asmā'* [the attributes] is that which has acquired a form. *Husnā* is a mystery, contained within the form called *asmā'*. Both of these together are called the *Asmā'ul-Husnā*. But if wisdom focuses within, if one will look within into the ocean of *'Ilm*, then he will find that *Insān* [true man] is the *asmā'*. It is the form of *Insān* which is *asmā'*. *Husnā* refers to the *wilāyats* of Allah which are His grace. His *wilāyats* or *husnā* are contained within the form of man called *asmā'*. *'Ilm* is that which can understand the *husnā* which is the

---

[17] In Arabic all letters are consonants, and the vowels or lack of vowels are indicated by diacritical marks placed above or below the letter. The *fathah* indicates the sound 'a' and the *sukoon* denotes a vowelless consonant. Thus, *lām sukoon* would be silent without the preceeding sound of *alif* with *fathah*. In analogy, man's heart would be silent without the connection to the resonance of God.

Qur'an. *'Ilm* can understand its actions, its meaning, its mystery, the limitless grace and the incomparable love. That is *'Ilm*. Only one who has known and understood *'Ilm* will know Allah. He is the one who can know Allah and truly pray to Him. He will have the same qualities, actions, and conduct as God.

Now, look at the ocean. The ocean is a vast expanse of water which surrounds the earth. If we take a drop of water out of that, will the size of the ocean be reduced? If we swim from one shore to the other, we could win a prize, but is that of any benefit to us? If we travel in a ship from one country to another, is it of any benefit to us? We may receive a certificate, but that is all. Because you are concerned with the section of creation, because you desire it and spend your time studying it, you may win a certificate for your knowledge of these *sifāts*, which are only examples. You may win a certificate, or a medal, or a title. That is all you will get. Nothing more. But for that other level of knowledge, you need to direct your *qalb* upwards. This is why the Prophet, *Nabī Muhammad Mustafā (Sal.)*, [18] has said, "Go even unto China and search for *'Ilm*." We must understand that. Only if we succeed in

---

[18] *Nabī Muhammad Mustafā*: Muhammad, the Chosen Prophet (*Sal.*).

understanding and acquiring that *'Ilm* will we be able to understand, learn about, and swim in the vast ocean which is the heart of man, the *qalb* of *Insān*. The *qalb* of *Insān* is a vast ocean which no one can swim across. It is a vast universe. His *qalb* is a net from which man is unable to extricate himself. It is an ocean full of magnetic currents that keeps pulling him without letting him go. It pulls him by performing four hundred trillion, ten thousand miracles. Wherever it takes hold, it makes man look down toward the section of the creation, toward the *sifāt*.

But at the stage when one has understood the meaning of *'Ilm*, if he opens that ocean of the *qalb* and looks within, he will see only Allah's grace, His *wilāyat*, His sound, His resonance, His explanations, His action, His conduct, His speech, His incomparable love, His limitless grace, and undiminishing wealth—everything will be within that *qalb*. His grace, His mystery, all these can be understood only through *'Ilm*. Absolute faith [*Īmān*] can be understood only through faith. Patience [*saboor*] can be understood only through patience. Contentment [*shukoor*] can be understood only through contentment. Absolute trust [*tawakkul*] can be understood only through that trust. And finally *Alhamdulillāh*—His praise can be understood only through His praise. Only the *Kalimah* can understand the *Kalimah*.[19] Prayer [*salawāt*] can be understood only through prayer. And *salaams* [greetings of peace] can be understood only through *salaams*.

For anything that we see on the outside, there is something corresponding to it within. We see the eye, do we not? But what can the eye do by itself? We see only the eye, but there is a light within the eye; there is an eye within the eye. We see a scene, a physical vision, and within that vision we see colors and glitters, do we not? In the same way, within each thing that we observe, we must see something else within it. That is the section of the *'Ilm*. Do we see the speech within the tongue? We see the tongue, no doubt. But within that, we see the speech and the taste. Within that taste, we find happiness, and within that happiness, we find beauty. Like this, there is something to learn within everything that we see or experience. The meaning of the *Asmā'ul-Husnā* is like this, and it is only through *'Ilm* that we can know that inner beauty.

---

[19] The *Kalimah* is the recitation or remembrance of God which cuts away the influence of the five elements (earth, fire, water, air, and ether) and which washes away all the karma that has accumulated from the very beginning up until now, and purifies the heart.

Lā ilāha ill Allāhu: There is nothing other than You, O God. Only You, O God.

153

GLORIFY ALLAH WITH EVERY BREATH

The world has written many different things about the *Asmā'ul-Husnā* of Allah. Many, many people have tried to describe these 99 names in a vast array of books. But that secret of the created form which is the *asmā'* and the *husnā* which is the *Zāt* contained within the *asmā'* were fashioned by Allah long, long ago. Every one of these names is a book. He has given these books into each person's hand and into each person's heart, asking them to understand these words. It is contained within the *qalb* of every being! We have forgotten these books that He has given to each of us, have we not? Let us consider this a little further, and once again make an effort to know this *Asmā'ul-Husnā*.

Now it is sometimes written: "Recite this name of Allah 3,000 times and you will receive such and such benefits. Recite this other name 7,000 times and you will receive such and such benefits. Or recite another name 6,000 times for these benefits. Recite this name 7,000 times and you will be cured of illness; or this other name 10,000 times and you will have a baby. Or say this name 15,000 times and you will receive some powers. Or recite this name 40,000 times daily for three months and all your difficulties will be erased and then you can become a king or a leader of your country." We have seen such things written in books. But this is not the *husnā*. All the above benefits relate to creation.

For what purpose are we suppose to recite these names? For what purpose do they tell us to shout in the supermarket? It is to buy the market produce that we desire in our minds. Why do we shout at the butcher's stall? To buy meat. Why do you go and shout at the cloth shop? To buy good fabrics. There is no purpose in reciting His name in the above mentioned fashion. The real value of these names is to glorify Allah every second. The *qalb* must be directed upward. The *qalb* that is directed downward toward creation must be turned upward and the sound sent upward. If the *qalb* turns upward, then this world of creation, this *dunyā*, is cut off. Cut away the sound of this world, this *sukoon*, and add on the sound of the *fathah* on top. This is how you must carry on. When you do it in this fashion, there is nothing in this world that you will need to ask for.

Allah has said, "I have given all of everything to man. I have handed over to him the 99 glorious names, all but one of my 3,000 divine attributes, my kingdom, and all of my wealth. Now, it is for him to use these. Man can utilize these in any way he thinks best." God has given everything to us. Now it is our responsibility to decide what belongs to us and take it. There is nothing that we need ask from Him. What are we going to ask Him for, when He has given us everything? There is nothing to ask. It remains only for us to realize our fault in wasting

the treasure that God has given to us and to improve
ourselves. He has given us everything. It is our duty
to realize what is right and wrong, what is good and
bad, and to take up that which is right and correct
ourselves.

There is the essence and the manifestation [*Zāt*
and *sifāt*], right and wrong [*khair* and *sharr*], heav-
en and hell. There is the world of the souls [*awwal*],
the world of form [*dunyā*], and the world of the
hereafter [*ākhir*]. There are good actions and bad
actions, good and evil. God has said, "I have given
all this to man. I have given him the 18,000 universes. I have given him that which is *halaal* and
that which is *haraam*. I have given over to him all
My wealth. So, whose is it to use? If he holds everything within himself and if he wastes the wealth
that has been given to him, what is there for him to
ask from Me? Nothing."

God has given you everything that He had. He
has already given everything to you except the one
attribute that remains within Him. If you understand everything that has been given you, then you
will realize that Allah alone is your wealth. And
when you understand this, you will realize that
there is nothing more you can ask for. Then you will
turn your *qalb* towards Him. And as soon as you
turn towards Him you will say, "You, Allah, are my
wealth. You are my treasure. You alone!" As soon
as you turn your heart towards Him, your very

breath, your speech, your blood, your thoughts, everything shrinks to insignificance, and you will be in direct communion with God. That state is *'Ilm*. *'Ilm* is the most excellent and most valuable treasure that comes of His grace. We have to reflect and understand this.

You may recite His names 1,000 times for this, 7,000 times for that, and 8,000 times for the other, but even if you recite it 50,000 times you will not receive anything. Why? Because He has already given everything to you. You have only to open that treasury within your *qalbs* and take out what has already been given. If you open your *qalb* and look within, you will find it there. If you open your *'Ilm*, you will find it there. But if you open places other than the *qalb* or *'Ilm*, like false wisdom and ignorance, illusion and hypnotic torpor, earth, gold and possessions, blood-ties and attachments, desires and mind, what will you find? If you open out a dog, what will you find? Only the smell of the dog. If you open a bull, what do you expect to find? Only the smell of the bull. If you open a goat what will you find? The fetid smell of a goat. And if you open out a fish, you will get only the smell of the fish. You keep opening and looking at all the animals within you, so you find only their different smells. That is your fault.

Open your heart and look. If you open the heart, you will find what is called *'Ilm* within. And

157

if you open out *'Ilm* and look within, you will find the grace; then if you open the grace and look within, you will find the light of the *Noor*; if you open the *Noor* and look within, then you will find the resonance. If you open the resonance and look within, you will hear the vibration. If you open the vibration and look within, you will find his *wilāyats*. If you open those *wilāyats* and look within, you will find all His actions. If you open the actions and look, you will find His duties and His qualities. If you open those qualities and look within, you will find that all lives, all creations are paying obeisance to Him. If you open that and look within, then you will see the entirety and totality of everything is condensed and contained within. If you open that container and see within, only He exists there. Everything is contained within Him. That is what we have to understand. That is called the ocean of Divine Knowledge, the *Bahrul-'Ilm*. This we have to understand.

THE STORY OF JONAH

At the time Prophet Jonah (*A.S.*) was sent to the world to preach the commandments of God, nobody would listen to him, and nobody respected him. Then he appealed to God, "These people are not respecting me, nor are they listening to Your words. O God! Please examine their state and annihilate these people. This country is afflicted by evil."

Then God said,"Is that so? Then tell them, Jonah!"

"But when I try to tell them, they drive me away, O God!"

Then God said, "If that is so, then take whoever your followers are and go. Is there no one who listens to you and follows you?"

"Not one, O God!"

"All right. Then I will destroy this country, just as you prayed for."

"O God, in what way will You cause this destruction?" asked Jonah.

And God replied, "The skies will descend toward the earth in the form of fire. That fire will come rolling down onto the earth, and then everything will be destroyed."

And even while Jonah stood watching, the sky began to roll down in the form of fire. Jonah began to run for his life. He grabbed his wife and two children and began to flee for his life. He told them, "God is going to destroy everything here. Let us run."

They ran for the ocean, but first there was a stream they had to cross. He left his wife and one child on the near shore and swam across, carrying the other child. Suddenly, a crocodile snatched the child from his hand and carried it away. He turned back toward the bank and saw a tiger carry away his wife and the other child. He had lost his wife and both of his children!

Jonah continued on alone and crossed over to the far side and saw a ship standing there. He asked them if they would take him on board. The ship's captain thought to himself, "He looks like a nice person with beauty in his face and advanced in years." Normally, they did not take passengers on board the ship, for it was fully laden with cargo and there was no room; but since he looked like a nice person, with a face full of light, the captain agreed to take him on board. Then the ship sailed off.

Soon the ship began to toss and roll violently. In all the time that he had been sailing, this had never happened before, and the captain began to wonder. The lives of all the people on board were in danger. He thought that there must be someone on board who was a traitor to Allah. And if they eliminated that person, all the others could escape. So, he wrote the names of all the people on board and they drew lots. When they drew lots the first time, Jonah's name was drawn. Then the captain asked, "Who is it that bears this name?"

Prophet Jonah said, "That is my name."

But the captain said, "You do not look like you could be a traitor to God. There must have been a mistake. Let us do it again." But again Jonah's name was drawn. The captain said, "Even on the second lot, the name of Jonah was drawn." But he would not accept this. He said, "There must be a mistake. Let us do it a third time."

In the meantime, the ship was pitching violently. On the third draw, too, the name drawn was Jonah. Then Prophet Jonah came forward and said, "That name is mine. I am the traitor to God. I have been an enemy to God, and as long as you carry me in your ship, all these people will be in danger of losing their lives. Therefore, please cast me into the ocean."

But the captain said, "We cannot throw you into the ocean. You do not appear guilty of treachery to God. Let us try a fourth time." Even this time the name drawn was Jonah.

So, Jonah ran and jumped overboard. As soon as he fell into the water, he was swallowed by a whale. He stayed trapped within that whale's stomach for forty days, and by that time, the whale had such a stomach ache due to indigestion. It was running here and there in a great discomfort. Finally it retched and vomited, and Jonah was thrown onto the shore. There he found an arid desert, and the only things he could see were the vine of a squash plant and a deer. The vine provided the only shade. The sun was very hot. Jonah would sit under the scanty shade of the creeper vine and the deer would come to him, and he would draw milk from the deer to drink. Sometimes a piece of bread would appear and he would eat it, without knowing where it came from.

Months went by. Then came the sound of God, "O Jonah! Now you have a nice house. You have milk and food, and you are living happily. Is this what I sent you here for? To live comfortably? Go back!"

But Jonah said, "O God, there is no transport to take me back. How can I get there?"

But once again, God said, "Go!"

So Jonah went, and at the shore he found that very same ship, which took him back to the place where he had boarded it earlier. He got off the ship and saw his wife with his two children standing under the same tree. There was no stream now. Then he went up and asked his wife, "Have you been standing here all the time? Did the crocodile not carry away one of the children? And were you not carried away by a tiger?"

But the wife replied, "Nothing happened to us. We have been standing here all this while."

"Is that so?" asked Jonah. "Allah has commanded me to go back. Come let us go."

As they turned towards their city, he found all the people coming towards him, praising him as the prophet. They came and were shouting, "We accept you, O Jonah. O God! Please do not destroy us. We accept Jonah." They all fell at his feet and begged forgiveness.

Then he asked them, "How is it you are not all dead? How did you escape the fire? What happened?''

"As soon as you left, the sky came rolling down and everything became fire. The whole city was surrounded by flaming fire. Then the sound of God came, 'You did not accept My Prophet, and therefore, you must become prey to the fire.' We cried, 'O God, we accept You and we accept Your Prophet. Please save us.' And God said, 'All right. Then accept him, accept My commandments, and listen to what he tells you. I am the One who created you, who protects you and provides food.' Then we said, 'We have accepted God, and we also accepted you, O Prophet!' Immediately, the fire rose and went up to the sky.''

Then Jonah asked happily, ''Is that so?'' And he instructed them in the *Kalimah*.

Again the sound of Allah came, ''O Jonah! The reason for my sending you down as a prophet was not just to protect your wife and children while all these other people were left to die. You were so very careful to take your wife and children to safety. You are a prophet, and all these children are yours. Did you not understand this? They are all your children, your followers, and your brethren. But you asked Me to destroy all these people and took care only of your wife and children. And see what happened!'' And God said, ''This is not the right way. It is your speech and your discrimination that affected your *Īmān*. As long as you have discrimination and differences within you, they cannot accept you. Only when this discrimination and separation leaves you, will they be able to accept you. As long as you hold an attachment within you, truth will not accept you, and justice will not accept you. Understand this. All right, now how long have you been away?''

Jonah estimated, ''Forty days in the stomach of the whale, nearly six months on that desert island, and the journey back was nearly 7½ months!''

But God said, ''All that took only fifteen seconds! Your going on a ship, your journey in the stomach of the whale, everything took only fifteen seconds. Within these fifteen seconds you have been harassed and driven hither and thither. It is this wandering that you held within your mind. When you had so much of wandering within you, in spite of having My commandments, how could you expect them to accept you? You had so much freedom, yet you held selfishness within you. So, you were the first traitor to My commandments. You are the traitor who did not carry out the commandments of God, and that is why no one would accept you. Is that not so? So much happened to you in fifteen seconds. But within two seconds they accepted Me.

''I am not opposed to anybody. I am not an

enemy to any of My creations. My soul is within each of them, and their soul is within Me. When I look I see only one. I do not see two. But you see three. That is the difference.

"From now on, understand the weight and worth of *Īmān*. Understand what is the sheath of the *Kalimah*. Understand the commandments of God, and when you have accepted these, understand the preface to *Īmān*. The preface to *Īmān* consists of the absolute acceptance of God without the slightest doubt. Next, you must understand the preface to *Islām* [the state of absolute purity]. That preface is patience [*saboor*], contentment, and gratitude to God [*shukoor*], absolute trust in God [*tawakkul*], and the state of *Alhamdulillāh* [All Praise is to God]. This is the preface to *Islām*. If you had these states within you, everyone would have accepted you. But you did not have these within you, and that is why you arrived at this state.

"Therefore, O Jonah, from now on fulfill My commandments correctly and preach them to your people. You must know Me. You must be able to see My benevolent look, My qualities, and My actions. And these must be understood by your people. Only such a person can be called My prophet or messenger. It is those qualities and actions that cause them to accept you and Me. Understand this."

WITHIN THE *ASMA'UL-HUSNA*

We talk loosely of the *Asmā'ul-Husnā*. But when we open the ocean of *'Ilm* and look, we find that it is *Insān* who is the *asmā'*. *Asmā'* means *sūrat*, body, or form; and *husnā* is the *Zāt* of Allah which is within that form. *Zāt* is the explanation, His grace, His mystery. This *Zāt* has to be seen through the form of man, the *sūrat* of *Insān*, the *asmā'* which is linked together with the 28 letters. Within that *asmā'* is the *husnā*—His *wilāyat*. This is what needs to be understood, through the ocean of *'Ilm*. There is no point in just writing or reciting this. But in the way that the Rasool said, ''Go out and search for *'Ilm*,'' we must search for this Divine Knowledge which is the most wonderful treasure. That is *'Ilm*. What we have seen so far are writings about things that can be seen. This is merely a learning from examples. But that which came to the Rasool of Allah is *'Ilm*. That was impressed on the *qalb*. The words and powers of Allah being impressed on the *qalb* is true *'Ilm*. The *wilāyats* are those things which are manifested from within the *qalb*. And when the *qalb* is opened out, that is prayer and worship. We must understand this. If we really understand that station, then that is what is called the *'Ilm* of perfect purity.

My children! With the kind of knowledge that we have, we can never hope to reach a complete understanding of the *Asmā'ul-Husnā*, the 99 beautiful names of God. We need to use that 'Ilm to dissect every portion and look within. Out of the 99, if we take one particle, one *wilāyat*, and cut it into ten million pieces with the sword of 'Ilm, and then take one of these particles and cut it again into ten million pieces, and then if we take one of these particles and look within, we will find 99 particles revolving round and round without one touching the other.

Now, if you take one of those particles, cut it open into nine million particles and examine one of these pieces, you will see 99 particles revolving round and round glorifying God, without one touching the other. Now, after discarding all the rest, if you take one of those particles, cut it open into five million parts and take one of those particles and look within, you will again find 99 particles revolving around one another, without one touching the other. If you take one of these again and cut it 2½ million times and examine one of these parts after discarding all the rest, again you will see 99 particles revolving round and round one another — His *wilāyats*, His resonances and His sounds revolving round and round one another, one without touching another. If you take one of those particles and cut it into two million particles, one of those particles will show 99 particles revolving round and round, without one touching the other. If you discard all the others and take one particle and cut it into a million particles, if you examine one of those pieces, those 99 will still be seen revolving round and round one another without touching.

Now, if you cut one of those pieces into five hundred thousand pieces and examine one piece out of those, again you will see 99 particles revolving round and round, one without touching the other. Now, if you take that particle and cut it into one hundred thousand pieces... if you take a particle of a particle and cut it open, as you go on cutting and cutting it with *'Ilm*, the power within grows and grows. And when you cut and then look, that resplendence goes on revolving one without touching the other 99 by 99. If you cut one particle into fifty thousand pieces and examine one of those, they will be revolving as 99 particles, one without touching the other. If you take this and cut it into one thousand parts, and examine one of those, you will see 99 particles revolving round and round one another, without one touching the other.

The power within is too vast to be described. It will swallow you up. It will draw you in. Your form, your *'Ilm*, and your wisdom will fall senseless, dazzled by that power. Thus, that power swallows you and you swallow that power. This is the state of just one of Allah's *wilāyats*. But there are 99 *wilāyats* which are His actions, His conduct, His qualities, His duties, and His service. This is the state of the duties He performs. This is what is called *Asmā'ul-Husnā*.

'Ilm is that which can bring you into union and communion with God. When the heart is turned upwards towards Allah, it is the *qalb*. When it is turned downwards toward creation, it is a dog. We must understand this. When it looks down, it is the *kalb* [the Arabic word for dog], with its tongue hanging out all the time, drooling saliva. When the heart turns upwards, it is the *qalb* turned towards God. That *qalb* is the *Bahrul-'Ilm*, the ocean of Divine Knowledge. Man needs to understand what the *Asmā'ul-Husnā* means, but is it the dog that is going to understand this? No. When the heart is looking downward, it is a dog which sees only feces, dirt, bones, filth, corpses, and discarded things. This is all that the dog will go searching for. This is not *'Ilm*; this is the *kalb*. When the *qalb* looks upward at God, that is *'Ilm*. It is only then that all that we have studied becomes correct. As long as that state does not emerge within, and as long as we are a dog, a *kalb*, there is no correct learning. There is no *'Ilm*. That is the learning, the scenting, and licking of the dog of desire. But *'Ilm* is the Divine Knowledge that will understand *Asmā'ul-Husnā*, which are Allah's wonders, His grace, His wealth, and all the knowledge that has been given to man. This *'Ilm* has been bestowed to *Insān* in order that he may understand all this.

May God bestow upon you that Divine Wisdom or *'Ilm*. But you have to strengthen your *Īmān*. The strength of *Īmān* is needed, no matter what you set out to do. Every breath must carry your intention toward God. In your eyes, every look and every glance must contain the thought of Allah. Your eyes must understand right and wrong. The ears must know how to discriminate between wrong and right. The nose must know the difference between wrong and right. The tongue must discriminate between wrong and right. The taste has to discriminate between *halaal* and *haraam*. The body needs to understand the virtuous qualities of modesty, reserve, abhorrence of evil, and inner strength. The stomach needs to understand patience and contentment.

When every part of us really understands and does what it has to do, then that is the state of *'Ilm*. Then we will not commit evil. We will be turned toward God. We will have eliminated all that is wrong from our physical visions, and from then onward, integrity and the correct path will be revealed to us. Let us all reflect on this.

I have given a small meaning of the *Asmā'ul-Husnā*. Those who have wisdom can go higher and higher with it. This explanation belongs to the wisdom of an ant, a red ant, the tiniest of ants, the most rejected and most small of all ants. Those who have wisdom, those who are men, will understand the splendor of it. Those who have differences will not understand. Those who have what is known as the 'you' or the 'I' will not understand. Those who have the fanatical separations of mine and yours, my scriptures, your scriptures, my religion and your religion, will not understand. But those who have sacrificed [qurbān] these differences, those who have cut off these differences, will understand the qualities of Allah, and His compassionate duty known as *Asmā'ul-Husnā*. The *Asmā'ul-Husnā* are the duties which He performs. Please understand this.

Therefore children, please try to know this and understand that Allah is the primal cause. For this, faith, certitude of belief, unflagging determination, and *Īmān* are necessary. The whole world will come to fight and try to crush one who has this *Īmān*. Therefore, in order to cut off the qualities of satan, you must have the mighty sword of faith, certitude, and determination; the *Īmān* known as the tiger of the 'Arsh, the throne of God. Everything else must be severed away. This is what we must do. Please try.

May we all understand this Divine Knowledge. May God bestow His '*Ilm* on us. May God make His qualities to grow within us. May He help turn our actions into His actions. Let us strive with earnest effort to be obedient to His word. May we follow Him, His Rasool, and His *qalb*. Through this, may we turn onto the straight path, and perform that prayer directly to God. May He bestow His grace upon us.

As-salaamu 'alaikum wa rahmatullāhi wa bārakatuhu kulluh: May the peace of God, His gracious mercy, His bounteous blessings, and everything of His be upon you.

Appendix

EXPLANATIONS OF THE THIRD *KALIMAH*

BISMILLĀHIRAHMĀNIRAHEEM

The Third *Kalimah* that I have given to some of the children is this:

Subhān Allāhi
Glory be to God,

سُبْحَانَ اللهِ

Walhamdu lillāhi
And all praise is to God,

وَ الْحَمْدُ لِلّٰهِ

Wa lā ilāha ill Allāhu
And none is God except Allah,

وَ لَاۤ اِلٰهَ اِلَّا اللهُ

Wallāhu akbar
And God is greatest,

وَ اللهُ اَكْبَرُ

173

Wa lā hawla wa lā quwwata illā billāhi
And none has majesty and none has power to sustain
except for God,

وَلَاحَوْلَ وَلَهُ قُوَّةَ اِلَّا بِاللهِ

Wa huwal 'alīyul-'alheem. Āmeen.
And He is the highest, the supreme in glory!
Ameen.

وَهُوَ الْعَلِيُّ الْعَظِيْمُ

The meaning of this is as follows:
Subhān Allāhi: O God, You are the Almighty
One, the One who is the almightiest, the One who
is the greatest of the greatest. You are the One who
exists as praise to praise and as grace to grace, who
is endless and complete in all things, and who rules
all creations in that state. O God, You are the One
who receives all praises and sustains all creations
as the *subhān Allāh.* You are that One. O Lord who
is the creator and the recipient of all the praises of
all creatures, beings, and lives, all praises of all
beings are to You.

Walhamdu lillāhi: O God, You are that One
who is the highest, the One in whom there is all
peace, and for whom there is all praise. You are
that One who is the ruler, ruling with compassion
and tolerance. O God, You are the One who feeds,
protects, and nourishes all those praises and all

174

those creations. That is the explanation of *walhamdu lillāhi.*

Wa lā ilāha ill Allāhu: O God, You are the One who exists within the breath of all creations. You are there, moving within man's breath, both in his right breath and in his left breath, in each breath that he breathes. You are that One who exists and is understood as the breath within the breath. You alone are God who examines the word, the thoughts, the heart, and the look and bestows Your compassion according to the intention of each. That is the explanation of *wa lā ilāha ill Allāhu.*

Wallāhu akbar: O God, that light of Yours is the One which is resonating and resplending within all that You have created, and which is understood as that One absolute truth. All praises and all prayers of insects and all other beings, of things that move, and things that do not move are to You and to none other than You. You are God, to whom all worship is due. O God, You are the One who slashes the blemishes of the heart and the prohibited characteristics and actions of satan, and feeds with the good food of *Īmān.* That is the explanation of *wallāhu akbar.*

Wa lā hawla wa lā quwwata illā billāhi: O God, You are the One who is present within the left breath and within the right breath, within the truth, within the inside and on the outside, as the light within that light, as wisdom within wisdom, as

heaven within heaven. You are the One who protects, giving sustenance and nourishment to all of
Your creation. You are the One who protects all
lives without causing harm, the One who gives that
food without causing loss to any life. There is no
other God than You. As ruler, there is no other
ruler than You. As judge, there is no other judge
who can judge as You. And in performing duty,
there is no other One who can perform Your duty.
You are the only One who can perform that absolute duty. No one other than You can do that. O
God, there is no One other than You who performs
that selfless duty. You alone are Allah. You are that
only One. There is nothing in comparison to You.
You have no wife or child, no beginning or end. You
are the only One. You are the One without *māya*,
torpor, death, birth, end, or destruction. You are
the One who has nothing of His own—no blood-
ties, no hunger, no illness, no old age, no death, no
birth, no beginning, and no end. You are the One
who accepts the prayer of each and every being and
metes out Your judgment now and in the hereafter,
in this world and in that world. That is the explanation of *wa lā hawla.*

You are the One who resonates from within
and from without. You are the only One who resonates wherever You are, and You are everywhere.
You will be with those who deny You as well as with
those who accept You. You are the One who rules

over everything, having no form or figure. You exist as the rightful heir to the beginningless beginning and to the end. You are the truthful owner of the world, of the *qalb*, and of all creations. You are the One who is able to dispel the darkness and drive away hell, and You are the One who is able to remove these evil things and discard them. Through Your wonders You can burn all these illusions, *māya*, hell, mind, desire, satan, and all the satanic qualities of arrogance, 'you' and 'I', and the ego. Having burnt them, You reside there as eternity. Having destroyed all evil, all illusion, all satans, all magics, all devils, all satanic diseases, all animal qualities, the evil eye, desire, evil desires, *māya*, arrogance, karma, lust, miserliness, hastiness, intoxicants, murder, falsehood, lies, and all the other evil qualities and satanic influences, You will remain as the only One. You will remain as the only One, the only One who can display the glory and purity of Your truth. You alone are the pure One who exists forever and provides assistance, compassion, and protection in this world and the hereafter, in *awwal* [the beginning of creation], in *āthi* [the beginning of light], and in *anāthi* [the beginningless beginning]. That is the explanation of *wa lā hawla wa lā quwwata illā billāhi.*

Wa huwal 'alīyul-'alheem: You are the One who protects all Your creations from satan, the evil one who was cast out of heaven. You exist as the

One who protects all creation from the evils of this satan who is the constant enemy to man, the evil one who is ever-watchful for an opportunity to bring man to destruction and lead him from the path of truth to his path of eternal hell. O God, may You protect us from the evil plots and schemes of satan. Neither the schemes of satan nor of anything else can create, protect, feed, nourish, forbear, or tolerate as You can, O God. Your patience and tolerance have such power, O God. O God, who understands the speech, the thought, and the intention, who destroys the hostilities of satan and manifests as the radiance of Your truth in Your judgment—You alone exist in contentment in the *'Arsh* or *Dhahūt* [the throne of God] and in the *Kursī* [the seat of God]. You alone understand and administer the final day, the judgment day, and the creation day. There is none other than You, O God. That is the explanation of *wa huwal 'alīyul-'alheem*.

This is the explanation of the Third *Kalimah*. The Third *Kalimah* is that revelation that is called the *Subhān Allāhi Kalimah*. This was given by Allah to Isma'il, son of Abraham. At the time when Abraham was asked by God for the sacrifice of his son, Isma'il, God explained, "It is your heart that I want you to offer in sacrifice." The meaning of this is to sacrifice the evil qualities that are contained within the heart. These dark qualities exist there as evil sins, satanic qualities, evil intentions, base desires, and blood-ties. They exist as the sins of the senses, as evil smells, evil tastes, evil sounds, evil intentions, and as all the jealousy, envy, hatred, and all the evil that is contained within the heart. The heart is what has to be sacrificed; this is the sacrifice that will be accepted by God.

This Third *Kalimah* is the same *Kalimah* that has been given to the followers of the prophets, to be used during the slaughtering of animals for food, during the *qurbān*. It is only after reciting this *Kalimah* that an animal can be slaughtered for food. This is to be said so that the animal qualities, the satanic qualities within the animal, the blood of satan within the animal, the intentions of satan within the animal, and all other evil, beastly qualities present in the blood and in the bile may be cut off and destroyed.

The Third *Kalimah* was also revealed and explained to Prophet Muhammad (*Sal.*) for the purpose of destroying the beastly qualities within the *qalb* of man. For human beings it was given and is to be recited to sacrifice the evil and beastly qualities that are present within their *qalbs*. When a man slaughters an animal for food, this prayer is meant to destroy the beastly qualities within him that cause him to want to kill an animal. Although it is commonly understood that this *Kalimah* is meant to remove the qualities within the animal, if you kill the animal qualities within the man, then he will no

longer want to slaughter animals. Before the beast
that is inside man kills another animal, this prayer
was sent down so that both beasts could be brought
to a higher state. It is for these reasons that the
Third *Kalimah* was given to man.

EXPLANATION OF *QURBĀN*

If a person is to take food for himself, he must
remember that every life is the sole property of
God. And if he would desire a life that is truly the
property of God, he must first hand over all responsibility to God in *tawakkal-Allāh* [absolute trust and
surrender to Allah]. In that state, he must praise
the glory of God before slaughtering the animal.
This is one meaning of *qurbān*.

Allah has laid down certain laws for this. "You
desired this animal, this flesh, but you must realize
that this is also a life like you. You have not realized
this, and therefore, I am laying down certain condi-
tions or laws from which I hope you will realize
this." Allah passed these commandments down to
Prophet Muhammad (*Sal.*). In those times, about
1,399 years ago, people did not realize this state of
equality of life. Each individual would take a life
according to his own wishes. They would wring or
cut the animals' necks and slaughter them any way
they liked, each in their own houses or compounds.
Whenever they had celebrations or festivals, they

180

would sacrifice millions and millions of animals in order to enjoy their festivities. They would even steal animals from others, to slaughter and eat.

So in the time of Prophet Muhammad (*Sal.*), many people brought this complaint to him. The Prophet (*Sal.*) asked, "O God, what does this mean?" Then Allah sent down these laws or commandments which are called the *qurbān*. According to the commands of Allah, the people must not slaughter in this loose manner any longer. They must not take food that is *haraam* [forbidden], and they must take only the food that is *halaal* [permissible]. *Haraam* is mingled within everything you eat. There are evil things mingled into the body, and you must make them *halaal* according to the words of Allah.

In order to do this, God said that you must recite the *Subhān Allāhi Kalimah* three times before you slaughter the animal. While you recite the *Kalimah*, you must complete the severing in three strokes of the knife, one for each recitation. The knife has to be swept around three times, and it must not touch the bone. It must be extremely sharp, and the length is prescribed according to each animal—so much for a fowl, so much for a goat, so much for a cow, so much for a camel. Also, the animal must not regurgitate any food, and it must not make any noise; otherwise, it becomes *haraam*.

The person who holds the animal and the person who cuts it must always observe the five times prayer. Therefore, it must be the *Imām* and the *mu'azzin* who perform the *qurbān*, because very often they are the only ones who regularly observe the five times prayer. This also means that the *qurbān* must take place near a mosque where two such people can always be found. Before beginning the slaughter, they must first perform their ablutions, and then they must recite the *Kalimah* three times and feed water to the animal which is to be sacrificed. The neck of the animal must be turned in the direction of the *Qiblah*, so that the eyes of the sacrificial animal look into the eyes of the person who is doing the sacrifice. The person must look into the eyes of the animal and then, saying the *Kalimah*, he must cut the neck. And he must continue to look into the eyes of the animal until its soul departs, repeating the *Zikr* all the while. Then after the soul has departed, he must say the *Kalimah* once again and wash the knife. Only then can he move on to the next animal. He has to look into the animal's eyes, he has to watch the tears of the animal, and he has to watch the animal's eyes until it dies—hopefully, his heart will change.

Allah told Muhammad (*Sal.*), ''With this *qurbān* the killing will be greatly reduced, for where they used to kill 1,000 or 2,000 in one day, they will now be able to slaughter only ten or fifteen animals. If they started after the morning prayers, it would be ten o'clock by the time they are ready to begin, and they could slaughter only until eleven o'clock when they must prepare for the next prayer. In addition, it takes about fifteen or twenty minutes for each animal, because he has to wait until the soul has departed." This is how Allah instructed the Prophet (*Sal.*).

Then the people complained, "How can we do this? We can cut only so few! Our enjoyments and our festivals are being curtailed."

But Allah said, "Each one of you does not need to sacrifice one animal; you do not need to sacrifice one animal for each family. In place of forty fowls, kill one goat. In place of forty goats, kill ten cows, and in place of forty cows, kill ten camels. Sacrifice ten camels and then share the meat among the different families." So in place of four hundred animals only forty might be killed. The killing was reduced by that much. Thus, Allah passed down the commands to the Prophet (*Sal.*) to reduce the taking of lives. These are the commandments or laws according to the word of Allah, and this was the explanation in the Qur'an.

If you understand the *qurbān* from within with wisdom, its purpose is to reduce this killing. But if you look at it from outside, it is meant to supply desire with food, to supply the craving of the base desires [*nafs ammārah*]. Only Muslims and Jews (the followers of Moses) still continue to do the *qurbān* in this manner. Only these two people follow the law as it was handed down.

Man must understand through his wisdom, realize what is right, and if we can develop sufficient wisdom to avoid causing hurt and harm to other lives, then we will understand the meaning of this *qurbān*.

Glossary

(A) *indicates an Arabic word.* (T) *indicates Tamil.*

aham (T) The heart. Combining Tamil with Arabic, Bawa defines Muhammad (*Sal.*) as the *muham* [Tamil for face] and *aham*. Thus, Muhammad (*Sal.*) is the beauty of the heart reflected in the countenance. See also: *Ahmad, Muhammad, muham*.

Ahmad (A) The state of the heart, the *qalb*, or *aham*. *Ahmad* is the heart of Muhammad (*Sal.*). The beauty of the heart [*aham*] is the beauty of the countenance [*muham*] of Muhammad (*Sal.*). That is the beauty of Allah's qualities. This is not merely a name that has been given. It is a name that comes from within the ocean of divine knowledge [*Bahrul-'Ilm*]. Allah is the One who is worthy of the praise of the *qalb*, the heart. Lit.: Most Praiseworthy.

ākhir (A) The hereafter; the next world; the kingdom of God.

'alaihis-salaam (A) Peace be upon him! A standard supplication said after mentioning the name of a prophet or angel.

'alaihimus-salaam (A)   May the peace of God be upon them. The plural form of *'alaihis-salaam*, a standard supplication said after mentioning the names of prophets or angels.

'alaikumus-salaam (A)   May the peace and peacefulness of Allah be upon you also! The return greeting to "*As-salaamu 'alaikum.*" This greeting must be returned, otherwise a serious debt is incurred. See also: *As-salaamu 'alaikum.*

Alhamd or *Alhamdu* (A)   The *qalb* or heart of man; praise; the heart of praise. The five letters *alif, lām, meem, hey, dāl* which when transformed form the perfectly pure heart.

Alhamdulillāh (A)   All praise is to You. The glory and greatness that deserves praise is Allah. You are the One responsible for the appearance of all creations. Whatever appears, whatever perishes, whatever receives benefit or loss—all is Yours. I have surrendered everything into Your hands. I remain with hands outstretched, spread out, empty, and helpless. Whatever is happening and whatever is going to happen is all Yours. Lit.: All praise is to and of Allah!

alif, lām, meem, hey, dāl (A)   Five Arabic letters. In the transformed man of wisdom, these letters are represented as: *alif*—Allah; *lām*—*Noor*, the light of wisdom; *meem*—Muhammad. *Hey* and *dāl* correspond to the body of five elements (earth, fire, water, air, and ether), mind and desire, or the *sirr* [secret] and the *sifāt* [manifestations of creations].

Allāh (A)   God; the One who is beyond comparison or example; the eternal, effulgent One; the One of overpowering effulgence.

An'am Muhammad (A) or *Anna Muhammad* (T)   Nourishment or *rizq*; grace. It is Allah who gives nourishment or *rizq*. *An'am Muhammad* is the name for the
Rasool [Muhammad (*Sal.*), Messenger of Allah].
The *Rasool* (*Sal.*) is the nourishment for our *Īmān*
[absolute faith, certitude, and determination].
An'am. Lit.: The gentle one. See also: *rizq, Muhammad.*

anāthi (T)   The beginningless beginning; the state in
which God meditated upon Himself alone; the period of precreation when Allah was alone in darkness,
when He was unaware of Himself even though
everything was within Him; the state before *āthi*;
the state of unmanifestation.

Āmeen (A)   So be it. May He make this complete.

'Arsh (A)   The throne of God; the plenitude from which
God rules; also, the station located on the crown of
the head which is the throne that can bear the
weight of Allah. Allah is so heavy that we cannot
carry the load with our hands or legs. The *'Arsh* is
the only part of man that can support Allah. Hence,
His throne is on the crown of the head.

arwāh (A)   The world of pure souls, where all souls are
performing *tasbīh* [prayers of praise] to God; the
period when the souls were manifested and then
scattered all over.

asmā' (A)   Names; appellations; attributes; duties;
wilāyats.

Asmā'ul-Husnā (A)   The 99 beautiful names of Allah.
The plenitude of the 99 duties of God; the manifesta-

tions of His essence, the *sifāts* of His *Zāt*. The states of His qualities are His manifestations which emerge from Him. He performs His duty when these manifestations of His essence are brought into action. Then they become His *wilāyats*, the actions which stem from the manifestations of His essence.

The *Asmā'ul-Husnā* are the 99 beautiful names of His duties. They were revealed to Prophet Muhammad (*Sal.*) in the Qur'an, and he explained them to his followers. This is a vast *Bahrul-Daulat*—a very deep ocean of His grace and His limitless, infinite, and undiminishing wealth. If we go on cutting one of these 99 *wilāyats* over and over again, taking one piece at a time, we will see 99 particles revolving one around the other without touching. This applies to each one of the 99 *wilāyats*. This is the *Asmā'ul-Husnā*. As we go on cutting, we lose ourselves in that. We die within that.

How can we ever hope to reach an end of the 99. If we receive only one drop of that, it will be more than sufficient for us. The person who has touched the smallest, tiniest drop becomes a good one. These are merely His powers. If you go on cutting just one of His powers, it is so powerful that it will draw you in. That power will swallow you up, and you become the power [*wilāyat*]. Then you come to the stage at which you can lose yourself within Allah; you can disappear within Allah.

As-salaamu 'alaikum (A)   To say, "*As-salaamu 'alai-kum,*" is to welcome someone with respect. It means, "I am Islam. Among the creations of Allah, I am Islam." To return the greeting with, "*Wa 'alai-*

188

kumus-salaam," means, "I am Islam, also. By the grace of Allah, I am also Islam. We are one family of Islam. We are all the children of Adam. We live in the same place. We greet all with respect and love."

This is a greeting of love. *As-salaamu 'alaikum, wa 'alaikumus-salaam.* One heart embraces the other with love and greets with respect and honor. Both hearts are one. *Wa 'alaikumus-salaam.* I am also Islam. This is Allah's word. This is a word from Allah that reunites all in Islam. If one gives salutation, you must always return the salutation. Otherwise, you may incur a serious debt.

With this salutation you are acknowledging: 1) All of everything that was created is Islam; 2) All of mankind, every fetus born, is Islam; 3) God has said, "*Yā* Muhammad, I would not have created anything without you"; and 4) "Everything I have created through you is perfect purity and purity is Islam."

Lit.: May the peace and peacefulness of Allah be upon us.

āthi (T)   The time when the *Qutbiyat* [the wisdom which explains the truth of God] and the *Noor* [the plenitude of the light of Allah] manifested within Allah; the period after *anāthi*; the beginning of light; the time of the dawning of the light; the world of grace where the unmanifested begins to manifest.

awwal (A)   The creation of all forms; the stage at which the soul became surrounded by form and each creation took form; the stage at which the souls of the six kinds of lives [earth-life, fire-life, water-life, air-life, ether-life, and light-life] were placed in their respec-

189

tive forms. Allah creates forms and then places that 'trust property' that is life within those forms.

āyat (A)   A verse or sign of Allah. Out of all the revelations [*wahīs*] sent down by Allah, an *āyat* is a small sign, a small verse. An *āyat* is a verse in the Qur'an or in a *Hadīsz* [traditional story].

bahr (A)   Ocean.

Bahrul-'Ilm (A)   The ocean of divine knowledge.

Bismillāhirahmāniraheem (A)   In the name of God, Most Merciful, Most Compassionate. *Bismillāh:* Allah is the first and the last. The One with the beginning and the One without beginning. He is the One who is the cause for creation and for the absence of creation, the cause for the beginning and for the beginningless. *Ar-Rahmān:* He is the King. He is the Nourisher, the One who gives food. He is the Compassionate One. He is the One who protects the creations. He is the Beneficent One. *Ar-Raheem:* He is the One who redeems; the One who protects from evil, who preserves and who confers eternal bliss; the Savior. On the day of judgment and on the day of inquiry and on all days from the day of the beginning, He protects and brings His creations back to Himself.

Dars ul-Ambiyā' (A)   Lit.: The teachings of the prophets. This is a crown. It is said that Prophet Muhammad (*Sal.*) wore a crown called *Dars ul-Ambiyā'*. That is the treasure for the three worlds of *awwal* [the beginning of creation], *dunyā* [the world], and *ākhir* [the hereafter]. Every word of Allah is a precious gem, and all these precious gems, which were the words of Allah, were carried by the Proph-

190

et (*Sal.*) on his head. Allah gave this crown to Muhammad (*Sal.*). Every word of Allah is a precious gem which can never be destroyed.

daulat (A)   This has two meanings. One is the wealth of the world [*dunyā*]. The other is the wealth of the grace of Allah. The wealth of Allah is the wealth of divine knowledge ['*Ilm*] and the wealth of perfect *Īmān* [absolute faith, certitude, and determination]. If one were to fill his heart with only that limitless wealth of Allah's grace, then that is the *daulat* of limitless completeness and perfect purity for the three worlds of *awwal* [the beginning of creation], *dunyā* [this world], and *ākhir* [the hereafter].

Dhahūt (Persian)   The throne of Allah.

dunyā (A)   The earth world in which we live; the world of physical existence; the darkness which separated from Allah at the time when the light of *Noor Muhammad* manifested from within Allah.

fathah (A)   Arabic diacritical mark which denotes the vowel 'a'.

Furqān (A)   Islam. See also: *Zaboor, Jabrāt, Injeel,* and *Furqān.*

Gabriel or *Jibrīl* (A)   The angel which brings the revelations of Allah and through which Allah conveyed the Qur'an to Prophet Muhammad (*Sal.*).

Hadhrat (A)   One who owns the respect of the people, one who directs people on the good path, one who teaches the divine knowledge ['*Ilm*] that returns people to a good path — such a person is given the title of *Hadhrat.*

hadīsz (A)   In Islam, a traditional story of the prophets.

191

These are the words or commands of Allah which were received by Prophet Muhammad (*Sal.*) and the other prophets and were conveyed and demonstrated to the people; or the words of Allah that were given directly to the prophets without Gabriel as an intermediary. For example, when God asked Abraham to sacrifice his son, Ishmael, Allah spoke directly to Abraham. When Moses received the Ten Commandments on Mt. Sinai, Allah spoke directly. When Prophet Jonah asked God to destroy the city, God spoke directly. The words that God spoke directly, apart from the other words that He conveyed through Gabriel, are called a *hadīsz*.

Hadīsz Qudsī (A)   A direct communication between the Prophet Muhammad (*Sal.*) and Allah, without the medium of Angel Gabriel.

halaal (A)   Those things that are permissible or lawful according to the commands of God and conform to the word of God. This relates to both food and to knowledge [*'Ilm*]. See: Appendix—Explanation of *Qurbān*.

Hānal (T)   The second religion or step; Fire Worship; the Tamil equivalent of *Jabrāt* (A). See also: *Zaboor, Jabrāt, Injeel,* and *Furqān*.

haraam (A)   That which is forbidden by truth, forbidden by justice, forbidden by the warnings or commands of God. For those who are on the straight path, *haraam* means all the evil things that can be obstacles to them, the dangers that can obstruct them, and the actions and the food that can block them on the straight path. See: Appendix—Explanation of *Qurbān*.

Hayāt (A)   The plenitude of man's life; the splendor of the completeness of life; the *rūh* or the soul of the splendor of man's life.

Hayy (A)   The Life; the Ever-Living; one of the 99 beautiful names of Allah.

husnā (A)   The beauty; the beauty which is the inner form of man.

'Ilm (A)   Divine knowledge; the ocean of knowledge; the ocean of grace.

Imām (A)   Leader of prayer.

Īmān (A)   Absolute and complete and unshakable faith, certitude, and determination that God alone exists; the complete acceptance of the heart that God is One. For the five prefaces to *Īmān*, see also: *saboor*.

Īmān-Islām (A)   The state of the spotlessly pure heart which contains Allah's Holy Qur'an, His divine radiance, His divine wisdom, His truth, His prophets, His angels, and His laws. The pure heart which, having cut away all evil, takes on the power of that courageous determination called faith and stands shining in the resplendence of Allah.

When that resplendence of Allah is seen as the completeness in the heart of man, then that is *Īmān-Islām*. When the complete unshakable faith of the heart is directed toward the One who is completeness; when that completeness is made to merge with the One who is completeness; when that heart communes with the One who is completeness, trusts only in Him, and worships Him, accepting only Him and nothing else, accepting Him as the only perfection and the only One worthy of worship—that is *Īmān-Islām*.

Injeel (A)   Christianity. See also: *Zaboor, Jabrāt, Injeel,* and *Furqān.*

Insān (A)   True man; a true human being; the true form of man; the form of Allah's qualities, actions, conduct, behavior, and virtues. The one who has the completeness of this form, who has filled himself with these qualities—he is an *Insān.*

Insān Kāmil (A)   A perfected, God-realized being. One who has made Allah as his only wealth, cutting away all the wealth of the world and the wealth sought by the mind. One who has acquired God's qualities, performs his action accordingly, and contains himself within those qualities.

Islām (A)   Spotless purity; the state of absolute purity. To accept the commands of God, His qualities, and His actions, and to establish that state within oneself and to worship Him alone. To cut away the desire called *'ishq,* to accept Him and know Him without the slightest doubt, and then to worship Him is Islam. To accept *Lā ilāha ill Allāhu* [There is no God other than Allah] with certitude, to strengthen one's *Īmān* [absolute faith, certitude, and determination], and to affirm this *Kalimah*—that is the state of Islam. Also: the religion or creed of Islam.

Isrāfīl (A)   The angel of wind; the angel in charge of the element air.

'Izrā'eel (A)   The angel of death; the angel of fire.

Jabrāt (A)   Fire worship. See also: *Zaboor, Jabrāt, Injeel,* and *Furqān.*

Jabrūt (A)   The sphere of divine knowledge or *'Ilm;* the sphere of God's power.

jinn (A)   A genie, a fairy, a being created from fire.

194

kalb (A) A dog. That which lies in front of the station of
the heart [*qalb*] is the dog [*kalb*], the dog of desire.
If you chase that dog away and look within, then you
will find the heart of God [*Qalbullāh*]. If the divine
knowledge [*'Ilm*] and the perfect certitude of faith
[*Īmān*] are present, then God can be seen in that
place. But the dog has to be chased away first. As
long as the dog is there, Allah will never be revealed, nor will the angels or the heavenly beings,
for the dog will be barking all the time. The dog is
the form of one section of the qualities of satan. If
the dog is chased away, the heart will be open.

Kalimah (A) *Lā ilāha ill Allāhu*: There is nothing other
than You, O God. Only You are Allah. The recitation
or remembrance of God which cuts away the influence of the five elements (earth, fire, water, air, and
ether), washes away all the karma that has accumulated from the very beginning until now, and beauti-
fies and dispels the darkness of the heart and makes
it resplend. The *Kalimah* washes the body and the
heart of man and makes them pure, makes his wisdom emerge, and impels that wisdom to know the
self and God.

Karanam (T) The cause; the basis or support for all
lives.

karma (T) The inherited qualities formed at the time of
conception; the qualities of the essences of the five
elements; the qualities of the mind; the qualities of
the connection to hell; the qualities and actions of
the seventeen *purānas*: arrogance, karma, *māya*
[illusion]; *tārahan*, *singhan*, and *sūran*; the six
intrinsic evils of lust, anger, greed, attachment,

bigotry, and envy; and the five acquired evils of intoxication, desire, theft, murder, and falsehood.

khair (A)   That which is right or good, as opposed to *sharr* [evil or bad]; that which is acceptable to wisdom and to Allah.

Kun! (A)   The word of the Lord [*Rabb*] meaning, "Arise! Come to exist!" and with which He caused all of everything to be. Lit.: Be! Arise!

Lā ilāha ill Allāhu (A)   There are two aspects. *Lā ilāha* is the manifestation of creation [*sifāt*]. *Ill Allāhu* is the Essence [*Zāt*]. All that has appeared, all creation, belongs to *lā ilāha*. The One who created all that, His name is *ill Allāhu*. "Other than You there is no God. Only You are Allah." To accept this with certitude, to strengthen one's *Īmān* [absolute faith, certitude, and determination], to affirm this *Kalimah* — this is the state of Islam. See also: *Kalimah.*

lām (A)   The Arabic letter (ل) which correlates to the English consonant 'l'. In the transformed man of wisdom, *lām* represents the *Noor* [the resplendence of Allah]. See also: *alif.*

meem (A)   The Arabic letter (م) which correlates to the English consonant 'm'. In the transformed man of wisdom, *meem* represents Muhammad. The shape of *meem* is like a sperm cell and from this comes the *nuqat* or dot which is the form of the world. See also: *alif.*

Michael or *Mīkā'īl* (A)   The angel who is in charge of the element water.

mu'azzin (A)   One who washes the area for prayers in a mosque, fills up the water when necessary, and summons the people at the prescribed times of prayer by reciting the call to prayer.

mubārakāt (A)   The supreme, imperishable treasure of all three worlds (the beginning [*awwal*], this world [*dunyā*], and the hereafter [*ākhir*]). The wealth and the One who gives that wealth is Allah and nothing else. Lit.: The blessings of Allah.

muham (T)   Face; countenance. In combining Tamil with Arabic, Bawa defines *Muhammad* as *muham* and *aham* [heart], the beauty of Allah's countenance, or the beauty of the heart as reflected in the face. See also: *aham*.

Muhammad (A)   The effulgent face of God's light; the brilliant heart of grace; the essence of God; the messenger of Allah which emanates from Allah; the *Noor* or effulgence of Allah; the beauty of God's qualities which entrances everything in creation. There are three *meems* in *Muhammad*, and one is this beauty.

The common meaning for *Muhammad* is the last one of the line of prophets. But, in truth, Allah has said, "O Muhammad, I would not have created anything without you." That same beauty called *meem*, which came at the beginning, also comes at the end as the beauty of Muhammad. If something was not there at the beginning, it could not come at the end. See also: *meem*.

mu'min (A)   A true believer, one of true *Īmān* [absolute faith, certitude, and determination].

Nabī Mustafā Rasool (A)   *Nabī*—prophet; *Mustafā*—the chosen one; *Rasool*—the messenger. A name used for Prophet Muhammad (*Sal.*).

nafs or *nafs ammārah* (A)   The seven kinds of selfish desires. That is, desires meant to satisfy one's own pleasure and comfort. All thoughts are contained within the *ammārah*. *Ammārah* is like the mother while the *nafs* are like the children. Lit.: Person or spirit.

Noor (A)   The resplendence of Allah; the plenitude of the light of Allah; the completeness of Allah's qualities. When the plenitude of all this becomes one and resplends as one, that is *Noor*, that is Allah's qualities and Allah's beauty.

Noor Muhammad (A)   The beauty of the qualities and actions of the *wilāyats* [powers] of Allah. That beauty is the beauty of the face or countenance. See also: *Noor, Muhammad.*

nuqat (A)   Dots (used in text to mean a singular dot); a diacritical mark placed over or under certain Arabic letters to differentiate one from another.

Partiyā? (T)   Lit.: Have you seen? Bawa frequently puns on the Tamil word *partiyā* and the Arabic *Sūratul-Fātihah*. *Sūrat* said with two different Arabic pronunciations of the letter 's' can mean either 'chapter' or 'form'. So the literal meaning of *Sūratul-Fātihah* is 'the opening chapter of the Qur'an', and Bawa also explains it as 'the inner form of man'. To further this interpretation using the similar sounding Tamil word, *Sūratul-Partiyā* means, "Have you looked at your inner form?" By mixing the Tamil and Arabic languages with this pun, Bawa is differentiating between the outer Qur'an and the Qur'an within the form of man.

Qalb (A)   The heart within the heart of man; the inner

198

heart. Bawa explains that there are two states for the *Qalb* and four chambers. The four chambers are earth, fire, air, and water, representing Hinduism, Fire Worship, Christianity, and Islam. Inside these four chambers there is a flower, the flower of the *Qalb*, which is the divine qualities of God. It is the flower of grace [*Rahmat*]. In that *Qalb*, only His fragrance exists. The other four chambers are black; they are really the dog [*kalb*], the black dog which is the world and the thought of the world and the five elements. But Allah's truth and His fragrance is that flower of the heart. That is the kingdom of Allah's church or mosque. There are some who worship in the darkness and some who worship in the light. Those who worship within that flower worship in the light. One section is light and the other four sections are the night.

Qiblah (A) Externally, the direction one faces in prayer. For Jews the *Qiblah* is Jerusalem; for Muslims it is Mecca. But to face Allah while in prayer is the true *Qiblah*. Internally, it is the throne of Allah within the heart [*qalb*].

Qur'ān (A) The words of God that were revealed to His Messenger, Prophet Muhammad (*Sal.*). Those words that came from His power are called the Qur'an. The Qur'an is formed by the explanations of Allah's qualities, actions, and duties; the state of *'alam* [the universe] and *arwāh* [the world of the souls]; the states of His creations and of the prophets who came before and the prophets who came after. These explanations were revealed to the people, to the prophets, to the saints, the angels, the heavenly beings, the *qutbs*, the jinns, the fairies, and to all created beings in order to demonstrate and explain His qualities and actions.

This Qur'an also exists within the heart of man. The qualities which are God's state of truth, His duties and His actions—together these form the Qur'an. This can be seen on the outside and on the inside. What is seen on the outside are the commandments, but what is seen on the inside is the explanation of God's qualities and actions, His beauty, plenitude, and completeness. Understanding what is seen outside is merely learning from example. If it is understood within it will be called the essence of Allah [*Zāt*]. If one goes on studying and understanding from the outside that is *sharī'at*, while inside it is *haqīqat* or *ma'rifat*.

In this way, climbing step after step after step, and understanding within, we must climb one quality to understand the next quality and then transcend beyond wisdom. We must climb holding onto God's duties. This is the study on the inside. If we understand within, this is the inner Qur'an. If we recite the Qur'an from within, we will see Allah as the One, the One truth, the only One worthy of worship, and we will see only one family. But if we recite the Qur'an on the outside and try to understand it, we will see many meanings, many divisions, many states, and many differences. This is why the Messenger of Allah (*Sal.*) has said, ''Go even unto China to learn *'Ilm* [divine knowledge].'' What does it mean? One meaning is that we must learn wisdom from within.

qurbān (A)   Externally, it is a ritual method for the slaughter of animals to purify them and make them permissible [*halaal*] to eat. Inwardly, it is to sacrifice one's life to the devotion and service of God, and to cut away the beastly qualities within the heart of man that cause him to want to slaughter animals. See: Appendix—Explanation of *Qurbān*.

Qutb (A)   *Pahuth-Arivu*, Divine Wisdom, Divine Analytic Wisdom, the wisdom which explains; that which measures the length and breadth of the seven oceans of the *nafs* [desires]; that which awakens all the truths which have been destroyed and buried in the ocean of *māya* [illusion]; that which awakens true *Īmān*; that which explains the state of purity to the *hayāt* [life] in the same way that it existed in *awwal* [the beginning of creation]. The grace of the *Zāt* [the essence of God], which gives the *hayāt* of purity back and which makes it into the divine vibration.

It is also a name which has been given to Allah. He can be addressed as *Yā Qutb* or *Yā Quddūs* [the holy One]. *Quddūs* is His *wilāyat* [power or miracle], while *Qutb* is His action. *Wilāyat* is the power of that action. Lit.: axis, axle, pole, pivot. A title used for the great holy men of Islam.

Qutbiyat (A)   The wisdom of the *Qutb*; the sixth state of consciousness; Divine Wisdom; Divine Analytic Wisdom; the wisdom which explains the truth of God. The wisdom that is the *wilāyat* [power] of the *Qutb*. That which awakens all the truths which have been buried, lay hidden, or destroyed in the ocean of *māya* [illusion]. That which awakens true *Īmān*.

201

Rabb (A)   God; the Lord; the Creator and Protector.

Radhiyallāhu 'anhā (A) or *Radiyallāhu 'anhu* (A)   May Allah be pleased with her (*'anhā*). May Allah be pleased with him (*'anhu*). A standard supplication said after mentioning the names of certain followers of Prophet Muhammad (*Sal.*), and also after the names of others who did not live at the time of the Prophet (*Sal.*) but were also in the same revered state. Frequently abbreviated as (*Ral.*).

Rahmān (A)   The Most Gracious, Most Merciful; one of the 99 beautiful names of Allah. He is the *Rahmān*. He is the King. He is the Nourisher, the One who gives food. He is the Compassionate One. He is the One who protects the creations. He is the Beneficent One.

Rahmat (A)   God's grace; His forgiveness and compassion; His benevolence; His wealth. To all creations, He is the wealth of life [*hayāt*] and the wealth of *Īmān* [absolute faith, certitude, and determination]. All the good things that we receive from God are called His *Rahmat*. That is the wealth of God's plenitude. If man can receive this, that is very good.

Everything that is within God is *Rahmat*, and if He were to give that grace, it would be an undiminishing, limitless wealth. Everything that has been discarded from Him is the wealth and the treasures of the world. Those treasures can perish and be destroyed and are subject to change. The word *rahmat* can also be used for those worldly treasures that change with the seasons. But the *Rahmat* of Allah will never change for all time; that is why it is the greatest, most valuable treasure to anyone who receives it.

Rahmatul-'ālameen (A) The mercy and compassion of all the universes. The One who gives everything to all His creations. He makes them arise by saying, "*Kun!* [Be!]" and then He gives whatever they need and comforts and rules over them.

(Ral.) (A) The abbreviated form of *Radhiyallāhu 'anhā* or *Radhiyallāhu 'anhu.*

rasool (A) Apostle or messenger. One who has wisdom, faith in God, and good qualities. One who behaves with respect and dignity towards his fellow men. A *rasool* is one who has completely accepted only God and has rejected everything else. One who has accepted God's divine words, His qualities and actions, and puts them into practice. Those who from time immemorial have been giving the divine laws of God to the people.Those who have such a connection with God have been called a prophet [*nabī*] or *rasool.* The name *rasool* has been given even to the angels. *Rasool* is also used as a name for Prophet Muhammad *(Sal.).*

rathina (T) Lit.: The name given to the nine kinds of precious stones or gems. If you acquire the clarity of the inner knowledge ['*Ilm*] of the nine openings of the body [two eyes, two ears, two nostrils, the mouth, the sexual opening, and the anus], if you eliminate *māya* [illusion] and arrogance from each of these outer openings, then each opening is transformed into one of these nine precious gems. And the Divine Wisdom which understands this transformation is the effulgent gem within the heart [*qalb*].

Rathina is the precious gem that makes the inner being of each opening beautiful. The inner light of the eye is a precious stone. The true inner sound within the ear is another precious stone. Within this light there is another light. Within this sound, there is an inner sound which is the sound of God. In this way, there is one precious stone for each of the nine openings.

Not this nose, but the fragrance of God within is a precious stone. Not this mouth, but the speech that connects with God and the tongue which knows the taste of God is a precious stone. And the two openings below — if you know their inner nature, you will eliminate arrogance, craving, and lust, and that place will be rendered luminous.

The light that renders both openings pure is the precious stone for each. Those openings may display hell on the outside, but on the inside they show the light. If we destroy the outer and eliminate or annihilate the hell that is on the outside of each of these openings, then each of them will show the precious gems within. Together these become the nine precious gems and this is a name given to Muhammad (*Sal.*).

Rathina Muhammad — The Jewel Muhammad, the nine precious gems. God has said, "*Yā* Muhammad, I could not have created any being without you and these nine precious gems." When one has acquired these nine precious stones, then his beauty becomes comparable to the beauty of Muhammad (*Sal.*), the light of Muhammad (*Sal.*).

rizq (A)   Nourishment; food; sustenance; livelihood.

When Solomon, son of David, offered to feed all the creations in the world, he could not even satisfy the hunger of one fish. That fish swallowed everything Solomon had to offer, and still it was howling, "I am hungry! I am thirsty!" Solomon begged Allah to save him so that he, himself, would not be eaten. Then Allah sent down the tiniest fragment of an atom of food and the tiniest fragment of an atom of water. The fish was holding its mouth open in hunger, and as soon as these two dots went in, the fish closed its mouth saying, "*Alhamdulillāh!* [All praise is due to Allah alone!]" That is what is called *rizq*.

All that we eat is just straw and hay for desire [*nafs*]. The atom of nourishment from God is one, and that is *rizq*, in the food for *Īmān* [absolute faith, certitude, and determination]. That is also what makes the elements say, "I am satisfied." That is why the name *Anna Muhammad* was given. *Anna* is the Tamil word for food. *Muhammad* means the beautiful form. *Anna* is that *rizq*, the food of beauty. That food is the beauty that comes directly from Allah. What you strip away and discard from *rizq* is desire or *'ishq* (A). That food that came from Allah as nourishment is *rizq*. *'Ishq* is desire; that is the world.

rūh (A)   The soul; the light ray of God; the light of God's wisdom. Bawa explains *rūh* to also mean *hayāt*. It is also called life. Out of the six kinds of lives it is the light-life, the ray of the light of *Noor* which does not die. It does not disappear, it is the truth. It does not die, it exists forever. That is the soul, the light-life.

That which exists forever and has no death is the soul. It is that which has obtained the wealth of *mubārakāt*. It is Allah's *Rahmat*. It is called light-life. The other five lives appear and disappear. They are called earth-life, fire-life, water-life, air-life, and ether-life. The *rūh* is the light-life.

saboor (A) Inner patience; to go within patience, to practice it, to think and reflect within it. *Saboor* is that patience deep within patience which comforts, soothes, and alleviates mental suffering.

The next stage is *shukoor*, normally called contentment. *Shukoor* is deep within *saboor*, pacifying and comforting. Even deeper within *shukoor*, still soothing and comforting, is *tawwakal-Allāh* [absolute trust in Allah]. And deep within *tawwakal-Allāh*, giving comfort and contentment, is *Alhamdulillāh*—surrendering all responsibility to Him. There is nothing left in my hands. Total surrender. I have given everything, I am helpless, I am undone.

Saboor, shukoor, tawwakal-Allāh, Alhamdulillāh —these are the treasures of *Īmān* [absolute faith, certitude, and determination]. The wealth of patience is the preface to *Īmān* and is the exalted wisdom in the life of a true man [*Insān*]. To possess these five and to act by them are the five most important duties [*fardhs*] for *Īmān-Islām*. These five are the preface to *Īmān*.

Yā Saboor—one of the 99 names of Allah. God, who is in a state of limitless patience, forgiving the faults of His created beings and continuing to protect them.

sakti (T)   A force or energy. In Tamil, the word *sakti* refers to *Shiva-sakti*. *Sakti* is the consort of *Shiva* [both are deities in Hinduism]. In Arabic it is *Ādam* and *Hawwā'*, and in Christianity it is Adam and Eve. They are the one original father and mother, but they are given various names and meanings in the different religions and languages.

(Sal.) (A)   Abbreviation for *Sallallāhu 'alaihi wa sallam*.

salaam (A)   The peace of God. Greetings! There are many meanings to the word *salaam*. When we say *salaam*, it means 'in God's name' or 'in the presence of God'. In the presence of God, both of us become one without any division; both of us are in a state of unity, a state of peace.

salawāt (A)   Plural of *salāt*, prayer; usually used for the supplication asking God to bless the prophets and mankind. See also: *Sallallāhu 'alaihi wa sallam*.

Sallallāhu 'alaihi wa sallam (A)   God bless him and grant him salvation. A supplication traditionally spoken after mentioning the name of Prophet Muhammad *(Sal.)*. Frequently abbreviated *(Sal.)*.

All beings created by God have been granted peace or have attained peace because of Prophet Muhammad *(Sal.)*. Saying, "*Sallallāhu 'alaihi wa sallam*," therefore means: "In the same way that you gave peace to us, may all the people who follow the Prophet be blessed with eternal and undiminishing peace." This is another meaning for *salawāt*.

sharī'at, tarīqat, haqīqat, ma'rifat (A)   The four steps of spiritual ascendance:

   sharī'at—the realization of good and evil and the conducting of one's life according to the good.

tarīqat — unswerving and complete acceptance of the good and the carrying out of every action accordingly.

haqīqat — the realization of Divinity and the beginning of communication with God.

ma'rifat — the state of merging with God.

sharr (A)   That which is wrong, bad, or evil; as opposed to *khair* [right].

shukoor (A)   Contentment; the state within *saboor*, within inner patience; that which is kept within the treasure chest of patience. *Yā Shakoor* — one of the 99 beautiful names of Allah. To do *shukoor* with the help of the One who is *Shakoor*, that is true *shukoor*. See also: *saboor*.

sifāt (A)   The manifestation of creation; attributes; all that has come into appearance as form; that which arose from the word "*Kun!* [Be!]"

sirr (A)   The mystery of God; His secret.

Subhān Allāhi Kalimah (A)   See: *Third Kalimah* and Appendix.

sukoon (A)   A circle 'o'; an Arabic diacritical mark which indicates a vowelless consonant.

sūrat, sūrah (A)   A chapter of the Qur'an. Spelled in Arabic with a different 's' it means form, shape, pictorial representation, illustration, figure, statue.

Sūratul-Fātihah (A)   The opening chapter of the Qur'an; the inner form of man; the clarity of understanding the four elements of the body (earth, fire, water, and air), and the realization of the self and of Allah within. The *Sūratul-Fātihah* must be recited at the beginning of every prayer. Within man is the *Sūratul-Fātihah*, and within the *Sūratul-Fātihah* is the inner form of man. If we split open that form, we can see within it Allah's words, His qualities, His actions, His 3,000 divine attributes, and His 99 *wilāyats* or powers. That is the *Sūratul-Insān*, the inner form of man.

The *Sūratul Fātihah* must be split open with wisdom to see all these within. It must be split open by the ocean of divine knowledge [*Bahrul-'Ilm*]. Opening his heart [*qalb*], opening his form [*sūrat*], and looking within; having his own form looking at his own form, that is the *Sūratul-Fātihah*. What is recited on the outside is the *Alhamdu Sūrah*. The two meanings differ in this manner: the outer one is a meaning of *sharī'at* [the first level of spiritual ascendance]; the inner meaning relates to the essence of *Zāt*. *Fātihah*, literally, means to open out. That is opening the heart [*qalb*] and looking within.

tawakkal-Allāh or *tawakkul* (A)   Absolute trust and surrender; handing over to God the entire responsibility for everything. Same as *Allāhu Wakeel*— You are my Trustee, my Lawyer, my Guardian. *Yā Wakeel*, one of the 99 beautiful names of Allah.

Third Kalimah (A)   *Subhān Allāhi walhamdu lillāhi wa lā ilāha ill Allāhu wallāhu akbar wa lā hawla wa lā quwwata illā billāhi wa huwal 'alīyul 'alheem*: Glory be to God, and all praise is to God, and none is God except Allah, and Allah is most great, and none has the majesty or the power to sustain except for God, and He is the majesty, the supreme in glory.

A prayer revealed and explained to Prophet Muhammad (*Sal.*) to be said as a part of the *qurbān* to remove the beastly qualities of animals about to be slaughtered for food, and to kill the beastly qualities within man that cause him to want to slaughter animals. See: Appendix — Explanation of Third *Kalimah*.

Tiru Qur'ān (A)   Also called *Tiru Marai* (T)   The Original Qur'an; the Inner Qur'an inscribed within the heart. All the secrets [*sirr*] and the essence [*Zāt*] from the three worlds (the beginning of creation [*awwal*], this physical world [*dunyā*], and the hereafter [*ākhir*]) have been buried and concealed within the Qur'an by Allah. There, He has concealed the explanations of the essence of grace [*Zāt*] and of the manifestations of creation [*sifāt*]. There He has concealed the *alif, lām, meem*; these three are the *Zāt*. That is why it is called *Tiru Qur'ān*. (*Tiru* means triple in Tamil.) All of everything is contained within that Qur'an. All of Allah's wealth is contained there, and all His *wilāyats* [powers] are present in their fullness in the Qur'an, the *Tiru Qur'ān*.

Ummul-Qur'ān (A)   The 'source' or 'mother' of the Qur'an. It is used commonly to refer to the *Sūratul-Fātihah* or the opening chapter of the Qur'an. It is said that within the 124 letters of the *Sūratul-Fātihah* is contained the meaning of the entire Qur'an. It is often used to denote the eternal source of all the revelations to all of the prophets and is also known as the *ummul-kitāb* (the mother or source of the book). This is a divine indestructible tablet on which all is recorded. This is the silent Qur'an which exists as a mystery within the heart [*qalb*] of each person. See also: *Tiru Qur'ān*.

wahī (A)   Revelation; inspiration from God; the inspired

210

word of God revealed to a prophet; the commandments or words of God. *Wahīs* or revelations have
come to Adam, Moses, and various other prophets,
but most of all to Prophet Muhammad (*Sal.*). Muhammad (*Sal.*) received 6,666 revelations. All the
histories of each of the prophets were contained
within the revelations given to Prophet Muhammad
(*Sal.*).

wilāyat or *vilāyat* (A)   God's power; that which has been
revealed and manifested through God's actions; the
miraculous names and actions of God; the powers
of His attributes through which all creations came
into existence. See also: *Asmā'ul-Husnā.*

Yā (A)   A title of praise; a title of greatness and glory;
the vocative 'O'.

Zaboor, Jabrāt, Injeel, and *Furqān* (A)   The four religions or the four steps of spiritual ascendance. The
inner form of man [*Sūratul-Insān*] is made up of the
four religions. The four religions constitute his body.

First is the religion in which man appeared, the
creation of his form, the religion in which forms are
created. That is *Zaboor*, Hinduism. In the body, that
relates to the area below the waist.

Second is *Jabrāt*, Fire Worship. That relates to
hunger, disease, and old age. That is the area of the
stomach.

Third is *Injeel*, Christianity. That is the region of
the heart which is filled with thoughts, emotions,
spirits, vapors, many tens of millions of forms, the
five elements, mind and desire, and four hundred
trillion, ten thousand spiritual worships.

Fourth is *Furqān*, the religion sent down to Moses

and Muhammad (Sal.). That corresponds to the head. It is made up of the seven causes (two eyes, two ears, two nostrils, and one mouth), and it will give explanations through these.

To study these four religions as four steps and to understand them, to study the differences and understand the difference between good and evil, that is the head or *Furqān*. The head is the leader or chief for all four religions. If there is no head, the form cannot be identified. There are no identifying marks. It is the head that sees with the identifying signs. To see with the eyes; to hear with the ears; to smell through the nostrils; to speak or taste with the mouth; to give information and to explain through wisdom; to transmit explanations to the *qalb* or heart; to realize and understand the difference between good and evil; to take up whatever is good, to show it, and transmit the meaning to the heart—that is *Furqān*. The head of every man is called *Furqān*.

There are two meanings called the *Sūratul-Insān* and the *Sūratul-Fātihah*. It is the *sūrat* or the body-form that is man or *Insān*. The wisdom that is capable of inspecting and analyzing this body has appeared within him. Allah has given the essence [*Zāt*] to know and understand the manifestations of creation [*sifāts*]. Having known this, to take up what is good and discard what is evil—that is *Furqān*. These four religions form the body of man, and the religion of *Furqān* helps man to understand these. For divine knowledge ['*Ilm*] these are four steps, but for the intellect they exist as four religions. And

Furqān is that which makes this explanation complete.

Lit.: *Zaboor*—the religion given to David, the psalms of David; *Jabrāt* (*Jabrūt*) a stage in sufi terminology denoting the sphere of knowledge or station where one discards personal power and becomes assimilated into the power of God. *Injeel*— the Gospels; *Furqān*—the criterion of right and wrong.

Zāt (A)   The essence of God; His treasury; His wealth of purity. His grace.

Indexes

INDEX BY ARABIC NAME

Fattāh 18 • Opener of the Heart
Ghaffār 14 • Absolver
Ghafūr 34 • Much-Forgiving
Ghanīy 88 • Rich
Hādī 94 • Guide
Hafīz 38 • Preserver
Hakam 28 • Judge
Hakīm 46 • Wise
Halīm 32 • Clement
Hamīd 56 • Praiseworthy
Haqq 51 • Truth
Hasīb 40 • Reckoner
Hayy 62 • Living
Jabbār 9 • Repairer
Jalīl 41 • Sublime
Jāmi' 87 • Gatherer
Kabīr 37 • Great
Karīm 42 • Generous
Khabīr 31 • Aware
Khāfid 22 • Abaser
Khāliq 11 • Creator
Latīf 30 • Most Subtle and Gracious
Majīd 48 • Glorious
Mājid 65 • Noble
Malik 3 • King
Mālikal-Mulk 84 • King of Supreme Dominion
Māni' 90 • Preventer
Matīn 54 • Firm
Mu'akhkhir 72 • Deferrer
Mu'īd 59 • Restorer
Mu'izz 24 • Honorer
Mu'min 6 • Faithful

Mubdi' 58 • Originator
Mudhill 25 • Degrader
Mughnī 89 • Enricher
Muhaimin 7 • Protector
Muhsī 57 • Accountant
Muhyī 60 • Bestower of Life
Mujīb 44 • Hearer and Answerer of Prayer
Mumīt 61 • Causer of Death
Muntaqim 81 • Avenger
Muqaddim 71 • Foremost
Muqīt 39 • Sustainer
Muqsit 86 • Just
Muqtadir 70 • Possessor of Power
Musawwir 13 • Fashioner
Muta'ālī 78 • Supremely Exalted
Mutakabbir 10 • Self-Expanding
Nāfi' 92 • Benefiter
Nūr 93 • Light
Qābid 20 • Restrainer
Qādir 69 • Powerful
Qahhār 15 • Dominant
Qawīy 53 • Almighty
Qayyūm 63 • Self-Subsisting
Quddūs 4 • Holy
Rāfi' 23 • Exalter
Ra'ūf 83 • Kind
Rahīm 2 • Compassionate
Rahmān 1 • Merciful
Raqīb 43 • Watchful
Rashīd 98 • Unerring
Razzāq 17 • Provider
Sabūr 99 • Most Patient

216

INDEX BY EXPANDED ENGLISH DEFINITION

Names in bold denote the primary meaning.

217

222

224

226

228

229

232

TEXT INDEX

Numbers in bold denote primary references.

234

Treasures of the Heart:
Sufi Stories for Young Children

To Die Before Death: The Sufi Way of Life

A Song of Muhammad (Sal.)

Hajj: The Inner Pilgrimage

Gems of Wisdom series—
Vol. 1: The Value of Good Qualities
Vol. 2: Beyond Mind and Desire
Vol. 3: The Innermost Heart
Vol. 4: Come to Prayer

A Contemporary Sufi Speaks—
To Teenagers and Parents
On the Signs of Destruction
On Peace of Mind
On the True Meaning of Sufism
On Unity: The Legacy of the Prophets
The Meaning of Fellowship
Mind, Desire, and the Billboards of the World

Foreign Language Publications—
Ein Zeitgenössischer Sufi Spricht über Inneren Frieden
(A Contemporary Sufi Speaks on Peace of Mind—
German Translation)

Deux Discours tirés du Livre L'Islam et la Paix
Mondiale: Explications d'un Soufi
(Two Discourses from the Book Islam and World
Peace: Explanations of a Sufi—French Translation)

For free catalog or book information call:

(888) 786-1786

ABOUT THE
BAWA MUHAIYADDEEN FELLOWSHIP

Muhammad Raheem Bawa Muhaiyaddeen *(Ral.)*, a Sufi mystic from Sri Lanka, was a man of extraordinary wisdom and compassion. For over seventy years he shared his knowledge and experience with people of every race and religion and from all walks of life.

The central branch of The Bawa Muhaiyaddeen Fellowship is located in Philadelphia, Pennsylvania. It was Bawa Muhaiyaddeen's residence while he was in the United States until his death in December 1986. The Fellowship continues to serve as a meeting house and a reservoir of people and materials for all who are interested in his teachings.

Also located on the same property is The Mosque of Shaikh Muhammad Raheem Bawa Muhaiyaddeen where the daily five times of prayer and Friday congregational prayers are held. An hour west of the Fellowship is the *Mazār*, or tomb, of M. R. Bawa Muhaiyaddeen, which is open for visitation.

For further information write or phone:

The Bawa Muhaiyaddeen Fellowship
5820 Overbrook Avenue
Philadelphia, Pennsylvania 19131

(215) 879-8604
(24 hour answering machine)

E-mail Address: info@bmf.org
Web Address: http://www.bmf.org

If you would like to visit the Fellowship or obtain a
schedule of current events or branch locations and
meetings, please write, phone, or E-mail
Attn: Visitor Information.